Silent Talk

Silent Talk

Setting the Stage for Introverts to Thrive in the Classroom and Beyond

Heidi Kasevich

ROWMAN & LITTLEFIELD
Lanham • Boulder • New York • London

Published by Rowman & Littlefield
An imprint of The Rowman & Littlefield Publishing Group, Inc.
4501 Forbes Boulevard, Suite 200, Lanham, Maryland 20706
www.rowman.com

86-90 Paul Street, London EC2A 4NE, United Kingdom

Copyright © 2025 by Heidi Kasevich

All rights reserved. No part of this book may be reproduced in any form or by any electronic or mechanical means, including information storage and retrieval systems, without written permission from the publisher, except by a reviewer who may quote passages in a review.

British Library Cataloguing in Publication Information Available

Library of Congress Cataloging-in-Publication Data Available

ISBN 978-1-4758-5491-6 (cloth) | ISBN 978-1-4758-5492-3 (paperback) | ISBN 978-1-4758-5493-0 (electronic)

Contents

Introduction vii

SECTION I: FOSTERING RESPECT FOR TEMPERAMENT DIVERSITY   **1**

1. Navigating Extrovert Bias   3
2. Temperament and Character Strengths   17
3. Adaptability and Stretching   33

SECTION II: CREATING INTROVERT-FRIENDLY CLASSROOMS   **43**

4. From Participation to Engagement   45
5. Silence as Prelude to Talk   57
6. Parent–School Partnerships   69

SECTION III: RESCUING SOLITUDE   **81**

7. Benefits of Solitude   83
8. Quiet Spaces   97

SECTION IV: LAUNCHING QUIET INITIATIVES   **109**

9. Call to Action   111

Acknowledgments	117
Notes	121
Additional Resources and Support	131
Bibliography	133
Index	141
About the Author	145

Introduction

> The next generation of quiet kids can and must be raised to know their strengths.—Quiet Revolution Manifesto

"JUST SPEAK UP!"

I used to have such a fear of speaking up in class that I tried to hide from my teacher's gaze. The typical advice, "Just come out of your shell," never ceased to backfire; every time I heard those words, I retreated even further into the safety of my shell.

Ironically, it was one of the most dreaded experiences of my childhood that started to set me free. In third grade, I took the ever-overstimulating Halloween holiday by storm, wearing a carefully selected, somber yet silently powerful, pilgrim costume. We hosted what was widely acclaimed as the best party of the year in rural Massachusetts. I still cling to the memory of what it felt like to float in and out of the designated party areas of our basement, making guests feel at ease as they bobbed for apples or guessed the weight of a massive pumpkin. Who couldn't be a perfect hostess if not a pilgrim?

A few years later, as an introverted seventh grader in a large public school, I vividly recall yet another boost to my confidence. I remember my trepidation at the prospect of asking my science teacher to sign my beloved green corduroy autograph book. I shrank from asking him to do so, as my lab partner and I had broken a beaker during a science experiment earlier that year, and I had never spoken a word in class.

Terrified, I summoned the courage to approach him, distant memories of that Halloween party propelling me forward to his dark mahogany desk. Ever so quickly, he autographed my little book. I waited all afternoon to read his words quietly at home, hoping that he had noticed my more-than-perfect marks on his multiple-choice tests and preparing myself for the worst.

Once I mustered the courage to open the book, I read his message, experiencing a profound mix of both joy and fear. His simple sentence still rings true in my mind today: "Reach out, H.K., you've got a lot to give." I knew he was right, but as an introverted girl, it seemed as though there was too much risk in ever trying to do that.

As I see it now, his words were remarkably different from those that I had heard countless times before: "Come out of your shell." "Just speak up." "You're so shy." I felt that he recognized me for the person I was, and he found the right words to help me both own my strengths—and step outside my comfort zone.

HELPING OTHERS TO REACH OUT

Stories abound today of introverts of all ages who feel misjudged, overlooked, and undervalued, seemingly unable to stand up for themselves.

Do we really want approximately half of our students—those who have introverted temperaments—to think that they are "less than" their extroverted peers? Those who thrive on solitude for processing, decision-making, and recharging—and who tend to prefer one-on-one socializing as opposed to larger groups—feel as though they are not normal? Of course not. Surrounded as we are by alpha, daring, and gregarious leaders, it is all too easy to impose a one-size-fits-all ideal on today's students. How can we set the stage so that all voices can be heard—in their own way?

A dramatic shift in mindset is needed: one that is rooted in Taoism, from the sixth century BCE. The yin/yang symbol captures the way in which "opposites" are complementary and not diametrically opposed to each other (introvert/extrovert; calm/excitement; deliberation/action). The yin, the dark coolness of the earth, flows into the yang, the light warmth of the sun. They invade each other's spaces to create a dynamic, perfectly round circle. Understanding the importance of integrating seeming opposites to restore wholeness—and to ignite energy in the process—is at the core of the mindset shift that is required to ensure that optimal conditions for learning exist today. (See figure I.1.)

We can cultivate Quiet power—the strengths of the yin—in our communities to create conditions in which we can all be our truest and best selves.

Figure I.1. The yin/yang symbol captures the way in which introverts and extroverts complement one another and can create synergy through the power of their interactions. *Kati Haajanen and Esther Aitken*.

The goal is not to replace one ideal with another—say, the introvert with the extrovert—but rather to foster temperament-inclusive cultures where everyone can reach out in their own way.

TEMPERAMENT-INCLUSIVE TEACHING AND LEARNING COMMUNITIES

The aim of this book is to provide research-based strategies and tools for K-university-level educators to foster teaching and learning communities where introverts and extroverts are recognized for their potential to learn and lead in authentic ways. Students and educators who recognize the power of temperament are better able to leverage their individual strengths and collaborate effectively.

A temperament-inclusive classroom is characterized by a balance between collaborative learning and independent work, group work, and solitude. It is one that prizes varied forms of classroom engagement, such as quality of speech over quantity, deep listening, and writing. As we cultivate a culture of Quiet in our schools, we honor the learning styles of between one-third and one-half of our students, those who are likely to fall on the introverted side of the introvert–extrovert spectrum.

CHAPTER OVERVIEWS

I invite you to peruse the chapters of this book in a spirit of generosity for nurturing the diverse learning and leadership styles of all students in your classrooms. I have worked with over three hundred schools nationwide in the quest to illuminate the importance of personality diversity and to cultivate Quiet power in their communities. Personal interviews for this book are numerous, and the ones shared are just highlights from hundreds of conversations I have had with innovative and compassionate educators.

In Section I, "Fostering Respect for Temperament Diversity," you will learn about the biochemistry that leads you to self-declare as an introvert or extrovert, the strengths that correlate with temperament, and ways to flex your innate styles to attain meaningful and manageable goals. This is the essential information as you learn about yourself first, and then help your students to better understand themselves using the tools provided.

In Section II, "Creating Introvert-Friendly Environments," you will explore research-based techniques to foster the engagement and creativity of introverted students and to harness the productivity and creativity of mixed-temperament teams. A critical part of this section is cultivating strategies for partnering with parents and caregivers and creating a home environment that is not over-stimulating for introverts.

In Section III, "Rescuing Solitude," you will learn the importance of solitude in our noisy and distracted world, as well as ways in which you can be a change agent in creating quiet spaces in your classroom, cafeteria, faculty room, and on your school grounds.

Each chapter includes "Micro-Mindful Moments," which are designed to help you think more deeply about the content of each chapter. The questions mirror the subsections of each chapter, and they are meant to be provocative for you personally. Your own discoveries can be used as a springboard to collaborate with others in your community.

The final "Call to Action" chapter provides stories to energize you to take action in ways that are most effective in the context of your existing school culture. Shifting school cultures around norms involving leadership, classroom engagement, and solitude is a challenge, and these strategies help you to embark on this important part of the introvert movement. Essential questions include: What might inhibit a Quiet initiative in your school? What might support a Quiet initiative in your school?

QUIET LEADERSHIP

In keeping with the "Call to Action" finale, I share one of the most transformative comments from a teacher to an introverted student that I have ever read. This one was written by my own son's middle school teacher. It betrays a keen sensitivity to temperament and a deep-seated desire to nurture the ability to "reach out": "In his caring and understated way, he sets the tone for the class by combining seriousness of purpose, generosity of spirit, and a great sense of humor."

The message: You don't need to be loud to lead. People with diverse personality styles can lead, and anyone can acquire the broad range of skills and behaviors necessary to lead a group effectively.

Over time, and in the context of a temperament-inclusive culture, it's my hope that the students themselves will be able to set the stage for everyone to thrive.

Section I

FOSTERING RESPECT FOR TEMPERAMENT DIVERSITY

Chapter 1

Navigating Extrovert Bias

"To be yourself in a world that is constantly trying to make you something else is the greatest accomplishment."—Ralph Waldo Emerson

"COME OUT OF YOUR SHELL!"

In twenty-first-century America, introversion tends to be associated with negative traits, such as being *slow, passive, unadventurous,* and *antisocial.* Extroversion, on the other hand, is associated with being *dynamic, outgoing, bold,* and *charismatic.* The introvert is the loner; the extrovert is the "alpha dog." As a result, extroverts tend to be the ones who seek out—or are chosen for—leadership roles in our businesses, government, and schools.

In American classrooms today, educators often inadvertently create conditions where extroverts can thrive, often to the detriment of introverts. For instance, teachers might define class participation as the number of times students raise their hands in class. In some courses, participation can count for as much as 50 percent of a student's grade, with quantity rather than quality as the key determinant. When a teacher pauses for just one second between asking a question and calling on a student, the introverts in the classroom—who require more than a mere second to formulate a well-considered answer—are left behind when their extroverted counterparts quickly raise their hands. Under these conditions, extroverts are at an advantage because they tend to process information more quickly than introverts—and they thrive on the social attention that comes with speaking up. In this common scenario, a teacher might encourage an introvert to "come out of your shell," while an extrovert is praised for the amount of airtime they claim during class. (See figure 1.1.)

4   Chapter 1

It's more than the typical class-participation grade that negatively impacts introverted students: they can often feel overstimulated during a hectic school day. Students of different personality types interviewed for this book overwhelmingly agreed that they are constantly expected to be doing something—or going somewhere—and are discouraged from spending time alone. Extroverted students are more likely than their introverted counterparts to feel at ease with busy schedules, collaborative work, and crowded, noisy cafeterias. In fact, one-third to one-half of students who are introverts often feel "abnormal" for eating by themselves, staying at home or in their dorm on a Saturday night, or reading a book during recess. With heightened sensitivity to social and sensory stimuli, introverts require more "alone time" than extroverts to restore their nervous systems during the day.

When introverted students feel constant pressure to fit into extrovert-dominated school cultures, they often report feeling stressed out, anxious, or depressed. Without quiet times, they are susceptible to feeling overstimulated and exhausted, causing them to withdraw and turn inward, potentially withholding information that could be critical for educators (as well as parents and caregivers). Given these circumstances, Is it any wonder that introverted students all too often lose confidence in their ability to lead when they discover that they fall on the introverted side of the introvert/extrovert spectrum?

It's not just our students, either. Michael Godsey in "Why Introverted Teachers are Burning Out" cites a study that shows 51 percent of teachers leave the profession within five years of entering it, a statistic associated with

Figure 1.1. Introverts are frequently told to "Just come out of your shell," which often leads them to retreat further into the safety of their shell. *Kati Haajanen and Esther Aitken.*

an emphasis placed on constant social interaction.[1] For example, introverted educators interviewed for this book were unanimous in their dread of lunch duty: the expectation to be outgoing and bubbly in the dining hall is onerous for teachers who need recharge time in between classes to survive—and thrive. A couple of minutes in the restroom between classes simply cannot provide adequate recharging time for introverted faculty members. Burnout is a real physical and emotional consequence of the lack of quiet times and spaces in our schools.

CULTURAL ORIGINS OF THE EXTROVERT IDEAL

Why do we tend to expect a specific kind of personality for leadership, success, and even happiness in America today? In *Quiet: The Power of Introverts in a World that Can't Stop Talking*, Susan Cain couples the "extrovert ideal" in American culture—charming, charismatic, outgoing, action-oriented people who can talk to anyone—with the emergence of the industrial and media ages at the turn of the twentieth century, when many believed that you couldn't succeed in life unless you were a fast-talking salesman.[2]

Cain relies upon the groundbreaking research of cultural historian Warren Susman, who affirms in *Culture as History* that as America began to shift from a nation of producers to one of consumers; collective ideas about the ideal self also began to shift. "Personality" replaced "character," and with this shift came an emphasis on cultivating a dynamic, outgoing persona so as to impress bosses and friends alike: self-sacrifice was replaced with self-expression; the work ethic with the leisure ethic; integrity with charm.[3]

The charming traveling salesman had his counterpart in the dynamic actor, a larger-than-life personality who was expected to make a good impression with a quick wit and a keen ability to think on his feet. A New York City drama teacher maintains it was during the vaudeville era that America witnessed the rise of the actor as a charismatic extrovert who was "supposed to come out to sing and dance . . . working hard to be a dynamic personality." The transition from vaudeville performer to cinema actor solidified the extrovert ideal in acting. She adds, "There was a time with the rise of moviemaking . . . when vaudeville performers became movie stars . . . and those actors needed to be glamorous wherever they went . . . the life of the party who entertains every night."[4]

Why does this matter in our classrooms today? According to this theater educator, sensationalized movie actors of the Hollywood star system were—and still are—the closest thing to a royal family in America. The cult of the charming, dynamic, and charismatic movie star reinforces the extrovert ideal

Figure 1.2. The cultural origin of the extrovert ideal is connected to the rise of the Hollywood star system, which idealizes those who are charming, charismatic, and dynamic. *Kati Haajanen and Esther Aitken.*

in any organizational culture in America today, from schools to corporations. (See figure 1.2.)

ORIGINS OF EXTROVERT IDEAL FROM THE FIELD OF PSYCHOLOGY

The concept of the extrovert ideal has its roots in the field of psychology. The Swiss psychologist Carl Jung, with the publication of his 1921 work, *Psychological Types*, is credited with popularizing introversion and extroversion as personality types, defining the introvert as someone prone to self-reflective introspection.[5] And his definition of extroversion? According to Merve Emre in *The Personality Brokers*, Jung relied on the theatrical notion of creating characters to define the introvert's opposite, the extrovert, as someone who is constantly playing different roles to suit the changing circumstances of life.[6] As Sophia Dembling affirms in *The Introvert's Way*, it was the notion of psychic energy—flowing inward for introverts and outward for extroverts—that was the foundation of Jung's expansive definitions of introversion and extroversion.[7]

Carl Jung was not alone, however, when he identified "introvert/extrovert" as personality types, and his neutral definitions were soon overshadowed by the theories of two of his colleagues, Sigmund Freud and Alfred Adler. Freud was a highly influential psychoanalyst in America in the 1920s when he began to use the term "introverted" in a negative way. As Marti Olsen Laney explains in *The Hidden Gifts of the Introverted Child*, Freud associated the introvert's inward-turning nature with antisocial, narcissistic behavior.[8] Adler, founder of the school of Individual Psychology, reinforced Freud's theory by insisting that introverts are prone to feelings of negative or low self-worth due to their proclivity for solitude. In "Introversion and Medical Student Education," Bernard Davidson, Ralph A. Gillies, and Allan Pelletier explain that Adler connected introversion with an inferiority complex due to an excessive need for alone time.[9] These two theories served as a catalyst for a rise in prejudice against introverts in the mid-twentieth-century America.

By the 1950s, America was a society that prized verbal fluency and assertiveness over introspection and deliberation, and those who did not fit in were often treated with medication. The rise in the use of anti-anxiety drugs during this time can be traced to the pressure to conform to the extrovert ideal. Research shows that by 1956, one in every twenty Americans had been prescribed the anti-anxiety drug Miltown for the "affliction" of not fitting into societal norms as bold, alpha, and gregarious human beings.[10] Similarly, as recently as 2011, the *Diagnostic and Statistical Manual*, the DSM-IV, or so-called "psychiatrist's bible of social disorders"—a manual that reflects cultural norms—came close to pathologizing both shyness and introversion as disorders.[11]

IMPLICIT BIAS

An understanding of the way our culture values one personality type over another is an important step in helping us to identify our own biases, which are often implicit or unconscious. Imagine two fourth graders waiting in line at school to have their new books signed by a visiting children's author. One child is busy talking to everyone around him about how excited he is to meet the author and ask questions about the book. The other child is standing quietly in line, reading her new book as she waits to meet the author. Which one is more engaged? Which one is the better student?

As many of the interviews for this book show, it is all too common for educators to perceive the first student, who is more extroverted, as the engaged one, and by extension, the better student. By contrast, the second student, who has a more introverted personality, is pegged as lacking in interest, and thus, the inferior student.

Let's look at a more specific example of implicit bias against introverts in schools. Kelly Wickham Hurst, founder and CEO of Being Black at School, a national nonprofit advocacy organization that focuses on addressing the complexities of being a Black student in America, claims that she felt "incredibly vulnerable" when she decided to publicly share how she failed to notice a quiet, bright, Black girl in her class. Yet, in the interest of raising awareness about blind spots, Hurst admits in "Quiet Black Girls—And How We Fail Them" that she inadvertently "forget to call on" an introverted student:

> My student is incredibly bright and always turns in her work. She has straight A's; she occasionally struggles with a concept, but she works so hard that I don't bother worrying about her. She has become wallpaper in my classroom. I often forget to call on her during discussions, and critical conversations about learning. Some days, when I take attendance and she's not there, I fail to notice it and just mark her "present." I think back later to the class period: "Did I see Starre in class today? Hmm. I can't remember."[12]

Hurst reveals in a personal interview that there were hundreds of responses to her story. Many of the classroom teachers who reached out to her after she published this piece divulged that they unwittingly do the same thing: "I have not realized how I have harmed the quiet Black girls in my classroom. Now I see more clearly."[13]

These stories illustrate the way the mind makes automatic associations. As Banaji and Greenwald affirm in their book, *Blindspot: The Hidden Biases of Good People,* when the mind encounters any information, related information instantly comes to mind.[14] In this, we make quick assumptions about people based on traits we think we recognize. We might assume a behavior implies certain characteristics we see in ourselves or in people we know, and our brains then engage in a shortcut known as "stereotyping" to process that information.

In 1922, Walter Lippman first coined the term "stereotype" to describe the ways in which we conjure up images to categorize individuals we meet.[15] Often, these automatic associations consist of negative traits: "Introverts are antisocial." Yet, it is important to note that we can challenge our own stereotypes simply by pausing—for ten seconds or so—before we make such judgments. When we take the time to truly understand another's personality, we are more likely to find ourselves in a judgment-free zone—a place that is not dependent on outward appearances or the dominant culture's message about certain groups of people.

There is still a long list of words that lingers in our collective—and individual—unconscious when we learn that our friends, family, or colleagues are introverts. Let's explore the three most prevalent myths regarding introverts: they are *shy*; they *are antisocial*; and they are *slow*. In raising awareness about these biases, we set the stage for temperament-inclusive cultures where both introverts and extroverts can thrive.

COMMON MISPERCEPTIONS ABOUT INTROVERTS

Introverts Are "Shy"

From a layman's perspective, it is easy to equate introversion with shyness, even though introversion and shyness are not equivalents. On the surface, they can appear the same, such as engaging in the following "quiet" behaviors: eating alone; moving away from loudspeakers at an all-school activity; or hanging out with the same person at a party. In fact, introversion and shyness are cousins, not identical twins. To put it simply, shyness ("I'm afraid of what others will think of me if I make a mistake during class discussion") does not spring from the same source as introversion ("I need to take time to think before speaking up").

A quick judgment can have a negative impact on our students. In her article, "Unconscious Discrimination: How to Defeat Four Hidden Teacher Biases," Monica Fuglei cites a 2011 study divulging that children deemed "quiet and shy" were rated lower on intelligence and academic ability when compared with children described as "average and talkative."[16] Moreover, when educators counsel introverts to "just speak up," these students may become fearful of what others think of them if they make a mistake, and hence more "shy." In this way, the anxiety that fuels shyness can stem from the internalization of the expectation to be more outgoing in school, as Ellen Hendriksen avers in her 2016 article, "The Four Differences Between Introversion and Social Anxiety."[17]

In a 2019 article in *Psychology Today,* Laurie Helgoe explains that while social anxiety is reported more frequently in introverts than extroverts, this does not mean that all introverts experience social anxiety.[18] In fact, both introverts and extroverts alike can be "shy." A shy extrovert and a shy introvert may simply appear to be similarly "quiet," but given the diversity of their nervous systems (see chapter 2), they go through different experiences. It is possible that shyness might be an even more painful experience for extroverts than introverts since extroverts have natural preferences for seeking social attention, socializing in larger groups, and processing their ideas out loud.

In an effort to combat the stereotyping of introverts as "shy," a head of school in the Northeast teaches a life skills class to help his students better "understand what's happening to them as they grow and develop—socially, emotionally, and psychologically—as individuals." He affirms,

> We need to be cognizant of the different ways that people learn and not attach false credit or praise on folks that have a tendency to hold court and have confidence in their verbal skills to do that. Teaching students to understand how they learn and express themselves helps to lessen the fear of social judgment.[19]

With such life-skills classes, educators can normalize conversations about introversion and shyness and teach students to self-advocate when they might be labeled as "shy." Let's replace the label "shy" with the following statements: "I take it all in and don't miss a thing" and "I'm internally aware."

Introverts Are "Antisocial"

Multiple studies have found that people frequently assess others based on the amount of time they talk in a group. As Cain mentions in *Quiet*, talkative people are considered smarter, better looking, and more desirable as friends.[20] In addition, the need to recharge alone can make introverts more susceptible to "loner" labels. As Margarita Tartakovsky asserts in "Seven Persistent Myths about Introverts and Extroverts" (2013), we all too often express concern about those who are not verbally participating in high-energy "happiness cultures."[21]

An interview with a school librarian reveals that raising awareness about extrovert bias can help support the learning of our introverted students. As she says,

> Many of the teachers thought that a really bright and interesting seventh-grade student was "standoffish and arrogant." I had known him since preschool, and when a teacher articulated the idea that he was "arrogant and standoffish," a colleague and I commented that this was not the case: "We don't think that's it at all. He is simply comfortable with his quiet nature."[22]

What does it mean to be "comfortable with your own quiet nature"? In general, introverts do like to socialize, but they prefer to socialize differently than extroverts: introverts prefer the company of close friends rather than a large group of acquaintances, and they often feel the need to recharge their batteries alone after a few hours out at a large gathering.

Let's replace the label "antisocial" with the following statements: "I am comfortable being alone" and "I need alone time to recharge."

Introverts Are "Slow"

Introverts are often especially attuned to their environments and other people, observing what is happening around them with a keen eye. This approach, which is often mistaken for slowness, is markedly different from that of extroverts, who tend to talk about their ideas with others soon after those thoughts emerge. In extrovert-ideal school cultures, hesitation to verbally participate can easily be interpreted as a sign of disengagement, or even a failure to follow along.

A French teacher from the Midwest reflects on her own childhood as an introverted student, stating that "it used to just mortify me when teachers would put me on the spot right away when I really wanted to think more deeply about questions." She continues, "And it was the kids who were fastest at speaking who got the most recognition, which frustrated me for a long time."[23] It is not uncommon for teachers to equate hesitation to speak up in class with a lack of paying attention, rather than equating it with the strength of listening before speaking.

Another seasoned educator and leadership expert affirms that introverts are inclined to sift through research and ideas until they arrive at unique insights—insights that can only emerge from a lot of time spent thinking. He notes that with such time spent in a rich internal environment, introverts see things "fifteen degrees differently from the norm . . . and that fifteen degrees is so *exceptional*." He continues, "I think that deep wisdom emerges from the well of introspection . . . from sitting with things, just letting thoughts mulch, until, from their own timing . . . something is moved and they know when to take action."[24]

The mulching metaphor is apt. It's the mulch that allows plants to blossom in the spring. A high-school teacher from the East Coast puts it this way: "When you ask introverts to speak—with preparation time—they have *incredible* points to make. They are not daydreaming."[25] They are, more often than not, sitting with their thoughts and listening to others before sharing their ideas. This can be thought of as preparation time to turn inward, considering possibilities and relying on an inner compass, or time to observe, attempting to fully understand the meaning of others' words.

Let's replace the label "slow" with the following statements: "I weigh options before making decisions" and "I am prudent."

STRATEGIES FOR DISRUPTING EXTROVERT BIAS

How can educators become aware of their unconscious biases and encourage their students to do the same?

Let's begin with school culture. It is imperative to add "temperament" as a marker of identity in our schools' diversity statements. As a director of equity and inclusion from Northern California affirms,

> Often when people think of diversity work, they think that it is all about race and gender . . . and so we worked to help people understand that diversity actually means all different kinds of identities and that people have many different identities in their lives. And that was how we opened it up so that people could talk about introversion/extroversion, in addition to other markers of identity.[26]

In the classroom, an effective strategy to encourage clarification of biases and increase temperament awareness involves inviting students to write descriptive words or phrases that come to mind as they think about themselves or their friends as introverts or extroverts, as well as a third personality type known as ambiverts—people who seemingly possess a balance between extroversion and introversion. This activity should be done *before* students have learned about their own neurobiology (see chapter 2). These words and phrases can be written on separate Post-it notes, with participants placing their individual Post-its in the appropriate space on a wall or dry-erase board that has been set up as a Venn diagram, with "introvert" labeled in one circle, "extrovert" in the overlapping circle, and "ambivert" at the intersection.

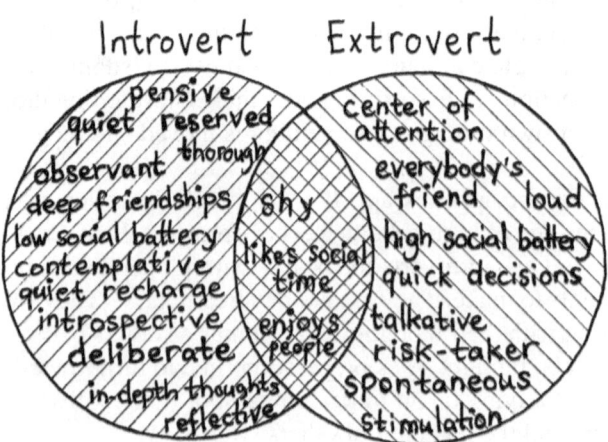

Figure 1.3.   When students are invited to share ideas about how they perceive introverts and extroverts, a new way of thinking can be created in the process. *Kati Haajanen and Esther Aitken.*

Once the Post-its are in place, ample time should be provided for everyone to read through the descriptions and reflect individually about their own word choices and placement. Afterward, the educator can lead a discussion about the students' choices of various words and phrases. Through open dialogue, opportunities emerge to rethink preconceived notions and build empathy. A new way of seeing others can be created in the process of this activity. (See figure 1.3.)[27]

Another educational approach involves asking students to share their interpretations of seemingly "introverted" behaviors, and then opening up a conversation about what this behavior might actually mean for an introvert. In this way, we can help students articulate a counter-narrative based in reality rather than cultural stereotypes. The following chart can help educators lead such classroom dialogues, as it explores six common misperceptions of such behaviors, followed by a positive counter-narrative to these negative interpretations. (See table 1.1.) It is designed to be a practical guide for deconstructing dominant myths about introversion.

With such linguistic twists, we can shift mindsets and broaden our understanding of what it means to be an introvert. At the core of any mindset shift is the practice of reflective pausing, which can lead to an appreciation for the authentic personality style of every person. Such pausing—via questioning or silence—serves as the foundation for cognitive empathy, our ability to identify and understand other people's emotions. As a Los Angeles-based actor, writer, director, and acting coach reassures us, "One of the greatest projects

Table 1.1. Common Misperceptions and Counter Narratives

Action	Common Misperceptions	Counter Narrative
Letting others speak up first.	Shy	Takes it all in and doesn't miss a thing. Internally aware.
Eating alone in the cafeteria.	Anti-Social	Needs alone time to recharge. Comfortable being alone.
Pausing, taking time to respond to a question.	Slow	Thinks through concepts, analyzing them so as to provide an in-depth answer. Prudent.
Not immediately involved and excited to be on a team.	Passive	Takes time to observe the situation and decide how best to be involved.
Taking time to make a decision.	Unadventurous/Risk-adverse	Consider options before taking action.
Working alone in a cubby in the library.	Loner	Needs alone time to focus on a task or project.

we have as humans on earth is to engage in our empathy and to experience, as fully as possible, what other people's experiences are, so we can understand and respond with informed compassion."[28]

A critical way to nurture empathy and inspire students to take action to benefit others is to teach them about the neurobiology of introversion and extroversion. We will explore this topic, as well as the character strengths of introverts, in chapter 2.

REFLECTIONS: MICRO-MINDFUL MOMENTS

"Silence is only frightening to people who are compulsively verbalizing."—William S. Burroughs

THE EXTROVERT IDEAL

1. To what extent does your school or organization favor bold talkers over reflective listeners as school leaders?
2. To what extent does your school or organization prize action and stimulation over deliberation and solitude?
3. To what extent does your school or organization require constant collaboration in open spaces?

IMPLICIT BIAS

We are conditioned to make decisions about others based on what we perceive as safe or comfortable. The first step to overcoming biases is acknowledging them.

1. Do you have biases that are limiting how you communicate with introverts in your classroom?
2. Have you experienced or observed extrovert bias in your school? If so, what are the consequences of this bias?
3. How can you set the stage for discussions about implicit bias against introverts in American schools today?

COMMON MISPERCEPTIONS ABOUT INTROVERTS

1. Sample Anecdotal Comment—"Introverts are shy":

    Erin never raises her hand to answer questions in class. I know she knows the answers, but she needs to participate in order to get a passing grade.
    - What does this comment say to the parent or caregiver?
    - How might you rewrite this comment from an introvert-inclusive perspective?

2. Sample Anecdotal Comment—"Introverts are antisocial":

    George likes to read a book during recess. He has a few close friends, but he should be playing kickball with the rest of his classmates.
    - What does this comment say to the parent or caregiver?
    - How might you rewrite this comment from an introvert-inclusive perspective?

3. Sample Anecdotal Comment—"Introverts are slow"

    During group projects, Emmanuelle is hesitant to offer ideas. By the time she has processed her thoughts, others have already spoken up.
    - What does this comment say to the parent or caregiver?
    - How might you rewrite this comment from an introvert-inclusive perspective?

DISRUPTING BIAS

Imagine two strangers sitting on a bench in a train station: he is eating a croissant while reading *The New Yorker*; she is feeding treats to her attentive service Labrador.

1. Which one is more trustworthy? Which one is more competent at the job?
2. As Mahzarin R. Banaji and Anthony G. Greenwald contend in their book *Blindspots*, there is no right answer to these questions, yet it is commonplace for people to pick one or the other, despite the fact that they know nothing about these individuals.[29] How might you use this example to teach students about implicit bias? Can you think of other examples that might illustrate the same point?

Chapter 2

Temperament and Character Strengths

"Knowing yourself is the beginning of all wisdom."—Aristotle

When we know ourselves, we understand better why we respond to others in the ways we do. At the same time, this self-knowledge allows us to become more aware of others' reactions to our behaviors. As a leadership educator affirms, "You have to start with self-understanding. Once we can understand ourselves and understand another, then we can do the work of interfacing between the two."[1]

As we invite students to learn more about themselves along the introvert–extrovert spectrum, we need to emphasize that temperament is just *one* of many identities, including gender, race, socioeconomic status, religion, sexual orientation, age, body image, and politics. As a middle school head asserts:

> Often people ask me, "What is the quintessential student at your school?" And my answer: "I hope it looks different. I hope there isn't just one kind of kiddo that would thrive in our community." We want to create a community where there are soft places to land for all kinds of students.[2]

That safe community with "soft spaces to land" can be created when all students are seen and valued for their diverse learning and leadership styles. Knowledge about temperament diversity, as well as the link between temperament and character strengths, is essential as we nurture the potential of all students. Over time, we become adept at creating classroom environments where students of all personality styles can flourish.

THE MYERS–BRIGGS PERSONALITY INDICATOR: PROS AND CONS

Let's start with the popular Myers–Briggs Type Indicator (MBTI), developed by Isabel Briggs Myers and Katherine Briggs, an American mother–daughter team devoted to Jungian psychology. Both Myers and Briggs were passionate about using personality traits and inborn gifts to help people find both satisfying jobs and happy marriages, twin goals that they linked to personal liberation.

Today, the Myers–Briggs personality test is used by almost all Fortune 500 companies and approximately two hundred million people a year. The test is a distillation of Jung's psychological types, and it defines introverts as those who gain energy from turning inward, such as sitting alone and thinking about things, and extroverts as those who gain energy from outward-facing activities, such as social events.

Witness the testimonial from a science department chair about the impact of the MBTI inventory on her life:

> I think the first time I actually labeled myself as an introvert was freshman year in college when leadership had us take the Myers–Briggs inventory. And so, that was the official moment where I said, "Yes, okay, I am an introvert." Before, I just would have called myself shy or quiet. And I've taken that test in a number of different situations—probably four times over the years at different organizations and companies—and I always score the same. I always come out as the same personality type which is introverted. So, this is a consistent part of my personality.[3]

While the Myers–Briggs personality assessment is an important tool in understanding the self, there is *more* to what it means to be an introvert than is revealed in the results of the MBTI. As Adam Grant asserts in "Say Goodbye to the MBTI, the Fad that Won't Die," introversion and extroversion have more to do with neocortical arousal, or the way our brains process the things we see and hear, than with a preference for social events ("energy-out" extroverts), on the one hand, or reading quietly ("energy-in" introverts), on the other.[4]

It's important to emphasize that both introverts and extroverts enjoy socializing; talking with others energizes both introverts and extroverts. The two groups simply like to socialize in their own way and for different lengths of time. Introverts tend to prefer one-on-one conversations with a narrow circle of friends, and they need to recharge alone after socializing. Extroverts, on the other hand, tend to prefer larger gatherings and often do not get drained by a full day of social events.

WHAT DOES IT REALLY MEAN TO BE AN INTROVERT? EXTROVERT?

For the purposes of this book, we will use a definition of introversion/extroversion that combines introverts' sensitivity to stimulation with extroverts' sensitivity to rewards. This definition is linked to a groundbreaking study in 2014 by Susan Cain's mission-based company Quiet Revolution and the cognitive scientist and humanistic psychologist Dr. Scott Barry Kaufman. They teamed up to develop an introversion/extroversion assessment that focuses on two key elements of our biogenetic natures—sensitivity to social and sensory stimulation, on the one hand, and sensitivity to rewards in the environment, on the other.[5]

INTROVERT SENSITIVITY TO STIMULATION

Introversion and extroversion fundamentally have to do with our sensitivity to social and sensory stimulation—crowds, bright lights, and loud noises, or even the taste of tart lemon juice. King's College Professor of Psychology Hans Eysenck's seemingly simple 1967 lemon juice test hypothesized that humans seek "just" the right level of neocortical arousal or the speed and amount of the brain's activity. In "Salivary Response to Lemon Juice as a Measure of Introversion," Hans and his wife Sybil reported that when tasting a stimulant such as lemon juice, introverts salivate more than extroverts.[6]

The lemon juice test is an enlightening activity that can be conducted easily in a faculty meeting or in the classroom to determine possible introversion or extroversion. While the results will not be based on hard science, the test is an entertaining way to help students and educators better understand the concept of sensitivity to sensory stimuli, and potentially, to self-identify as an introvert or extrovert. Follow the steps in the following chart to replicate the original lemon juice test.

LEMON JUICE TEST

Materials

Lemon juice, two Q-Tips per participant, and a scale that is sensitive enough to measure changes in the moisture content of Q-Tips.

Procedure

1) Put one end of the first Q-Tip swab on your tongue for 20 seconds.
2) Weigh the Q-Tip and record its weight. Discard this Q-Tip.
3) Squirt 5 drops of lemon juice onto your tongue. Swirl it around and then swallow the juice. Put one end of the second Q-Tip onto your tongue for 20 seconds.
4) Weigh the Q-tip and record its weight.

Results

For most introverts, the Q-Tip with the lemon saliva will be heavier, and for most extroverts, the weights will remain the same, showing that using lemon juice as a stimulant causes introverts to salivate more than extroverts.

"Lemon Juice Introversion Test," *Psychologist World*, https://www.psychologistworld.com/influence-personality/introversion-extraversion-lemon-juice-test.

After the Eysencks published their theory suggesting a biological basis for introversion, Dr. Jerome Kagan demonstrated in 1979 that sensitivity to environmental stimulation is present from birth and endures throughout adulthood. Kagan ran a series of experiments to see whether babies would exhibit signs of distress when exposed to environmental stimuli, such as the sound of popping balloons or the sight of a mobile swaying overhead. These babies were as young as four months. Kagan's studies revealed that about 20 percent of these children showed signs of distress when reacting to environmental stimuli, such as crying, arching the back, or kicking the legs. He labeled these children as "high reactives" and went on to show that the 20 percent who were "high reactives" were likely to develop into introverted teens.[7]

Continuing with Kagan's longitudinal studies, Dr. Carl Schwartz, a human specialist at the Developmental Neuroimaging & Psychopathology Research Laboratory at Massachusetts General Hospital, used fMRI machines to show that the high or low reactive temperament does not disappear in adulthood. In 1999, he found that "high reactives" were still more sensitive to pictures of unfamiliar faces, even into their early twenties.[8] In Quiet Revolution's podcast about the ways in which neurobiology shapes temperament, Schwartz declares that his numerous studies affirm that highly reactive two-year-olds, those more sensitive to novelty and outside stimuli, will continue to behave in a similar manner at age twenty-one. In other words, the two-year-old introvert who clings to his caregiver's side at a family gathering will mature into an adult who, by nature, prefers to decline an invitation to a birthday party after a long school week.[9] (See figure 2.1.)

Figure 2.1. Introverts are more sensitive than extroverts to social and sensory stimuli, and they prefer to socialize with a close companion rather than with a large group of friends. *Kati Haajanen and Esther Aitken.*

For introverts, too much stimulation can feel like Florence Nightingale's 1859 description of "noise" as a severe sensation of pain, as Marianne Szegedy-Maszak affirms in "As Noise Rises, so do the Dangers."[10] Due to such acute feelings of discomfort, introverts are driven to regulate their activity by acting in a variety of different manners: they may become shy (afraid to speak up or take action, as they are worried about what others might think of them), anxious, withdrawn, or timid.

EXTROVERT SENSITIVITY TO REWARDS

In "Why Introverts and Extroverts Are Different: The Science," Jennifer Granneman claims that while the brain's dopamine level is the same for both introverts and extroverts, extroverts have a more active dopamine pathway—or reward circuit—than introverts. This means that extroverts feel more energized than introverts at the expectation of rewards in the environment: making friends with new classmates on the first day of school, being the first to answer a question in the classroom, receiving a sports medal, or attending a lively social event.[11]

In their 2002 research on the main feature of extroversion, Michael Ashton, Kibeom Lee, and Sampo Paunonen propose that extroversion represents a high-intensity proclivity for gaining social attention.[12] As Scott Barry Kaufman affirms in "Will the Real Introverts Please Stand Up?" the main goal of the extrovert's reward system is gaining positive attention from friends and strangers, which may be affiliated with such behaviors as planning a party or telling a joke.[13] So, when extroverted students volunteer to share their ideas first with the class, they are likely experiencing a "dopamine rush."

In *The Introvert Advantage*, Marti Olsen Laney further explains that introverts may prefer to use a slightly different brain pathway, one that is activated by a neurotransmitter called acetylcholine. These two neurotransmitters, dopamine and acetylcholine, are connected to the two different sides of our nervous system: the sympathetic side and the parasympathetic side. When action is necessary, the sympathetic system, also known as the fight, flight, or freeze system, is engaged. Conversely, when calmness is needed, the parasympathetic system relaxes the body to conserve energy. While both neurotransmitters are associated with pleasure, the parasympathetic system, used more frequently by introverts, prepares one to withdraw from the outer environment, quietly reflecting. By contrast, the sympathetic side, preferred by the extrovert brain, is ready to take action and make quick decisions.[14]

WHAT IS AN AMBIVERT?

Children and adults alike often self-identify as individuals who fall somewhere along a continuum of introversion/extroversion. Those who fall in the

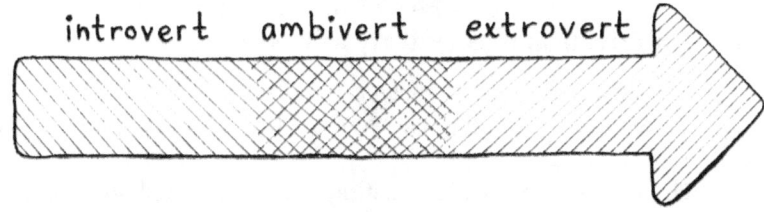

Figure 2.2. Individuals who do not self-identify as either introverts or extroverts often have difficulty discerning the difference between their authentic nature and their social persona (s). Further reflection about their innate styles—social, working, recharging, decision-making and risk-taking—often helps them to determine whether they are more introverted or more extroverted by nature." *Kati Haajanen and Esther Aitken.*

more central part of the spectrum are referred to as ambiverts. Some researchers, such as Dr. Adam Grant, professor of management and psychology at The Wharton School, contend that nearly two-thirds of people don't feel as though they lean toward extroversion or introversion, making them ambiverts.[15]

There are many possible reasons for self-identifying as an ambivert. First and foremost, it can be difficult to differentiate between our authentic nature and our social personas. Throughout life, our inborn temperament interacts with the environment, including familial and cultural norms and other markers of social identity, and we often conform to meet those norms and expectations. For instance, while a large family wedding might not align with one's preferred social style as an introvert, one might still plan a large celebration since it is part of the fabric of the social style of one's extended family. Second, we can flex our inborn styles, exercising our own free will (or free traits) in the service of personal or academic/career goals (see chapter 3). (See figure 2.2.)

That said, and despite the frequency of self-reporting as an ambivert, there is a *dominant* side to our temperament—introvert or extrovert—based on our sensitivity to stimulation and our sensitivity to rewards. The Personality Preferences Indicator in the next section is designed to help you and your students determine your dominant style.

INTROVERT/EXTROVERT PERSONALITY PREFERENCES INDICATOR FOR ADULTS AND OLDER STUDENTS

The following twenty-seven question temperament indicator provides a general understanding of personality styles. This Introvert/Extrovert Indicator has been adapted and reworked from several other personality quizzes with specific attention placed on the characteristics that students, teachers, and parents have found most revealing about themselves during school workshops on introversion/extroversion.[16]

Directions: Answer TRUE or FALSE to the Following Questions in Private and as Quickly as Possible

1. ____ People consider me to be an active listener.
2. ____ I like to take time to think about my response to a question before giving an answer.
3. ____ Unplanned phone calls sometimes go unanswered until I am ready to call back and talk.
4. ____ My favorite way to entertain is in smaller groups.
5. ____ I am a cautious risk-taker.
6. ____ I dislike small talk.
7. ____ I love to explore topics that I am passionate about over a long period of time.
8. ____ I am comfortable being alone with my thoughts.
9. ____ I can often feel drained after a couple of Zoom classes or meetings.
10. ____ My senses are keen, often reacting strongly to smells, foods, tastes, noises, lights, and weather.
11. ____ If my team accomplishes a goal, I would rather give credit to others than have the spotlight shine on me.
12. ____ While social gatherings with lots of people can be fun, I often feel exhausted after the event.
13. ____ People describe me as reserved and soft-spoken.
14. ____ I prefer independent work to group work.
15. ____ When entering a new activity, such as a party, I need to observe and survey the situation before joining.
16. ____ I can be easily overwhelmed when multitasking.
17. ____ I am content with having a few close friends and meeting with them one-on-one.
18. ____ I often freeze up when called upon and expected to give a quick answer.
19. ____ I prefer writing to speaking as a way to express myself.
20. ____ I prefer not to participate in competitive activities.
21. ____ I often choose to work behind the scenes to help others accomplish their goals.
22. ____ After a long and hectic week, I need some quiet downtime.
23. ____ I often notice details that others might not see.
24. ____ My best work is done in quiet, calm settings.
25. ____ I prefer lectures to participatory workshops.
26. ____ I often take my time to make a decision so that I can weigh the pros and cons.
27. ____I am hesitant to share my accomplishments on social media.

Results: If you answered **TRUE** to more than half of the questions, you most likely are an introvert. If you responded **FALSE** to more than half of the questions, you probably are an extrovert.

MODIFICATION OF INTROVERT/EXTROVERT PERSONALITY PREFERENCES INDICATOR FOR YOUNGER STUDENTS

A "Who am I? Cube" can help younger students articulate their personality preferences in a concrete and tangible way. Begin by inviting students to answer questions pertaining to their social, working, recharging, communication, and decision-making styles, with each answer placed in the appropriately numbered square of a simple paper cube template. Encourage them to use both words and drawings to personalize their creations, and then ask them to turn their answers into a three-dimensional art project.

The following six questions (one answer for each side of the cube) are based on the definitions of introversion and extroversion in this book—sensitivity to stimulation and sensitivity to rewards—and are designed to help students self-identify as introverts or extroverts. They can be modified as needed for different age groups:

1. What is your preferred name or nickname?
2. *Social Style*: Do you prefer one-on-one conversations with people you already know, or do you like group work and meeting new friends?
3. *Working Style*: Do you like to do your homework alone, or with people nearby and possibly a few partners?
4. *Recharging Style*: Do you need time alone after school, or do you prefer to meet with groups of friends when the school day is finished?
5. *Communication Style*: Do you like to think before you speak in class, or are you one of the first to raise your hand?
6. *Decision-Making Style*: Do you take time to consider your choices before making a decision, or do you make decisions quickly?

This activity is not only beneficial for helping students develop self-awareness at the beginning of the year, but it can also be useful at the end of the year as a conversation starter about what they have learned about themselves and others. One elementary educator, who designed the first version of the "Who am I? Cube" in 2016, advocates for making mobiles out of the cubes and hanging them in the classroom year-round. She has had great success with leading discussions about how students have "stayed the same" or "changed" during the year, with the decorative mobiles as a basis for these

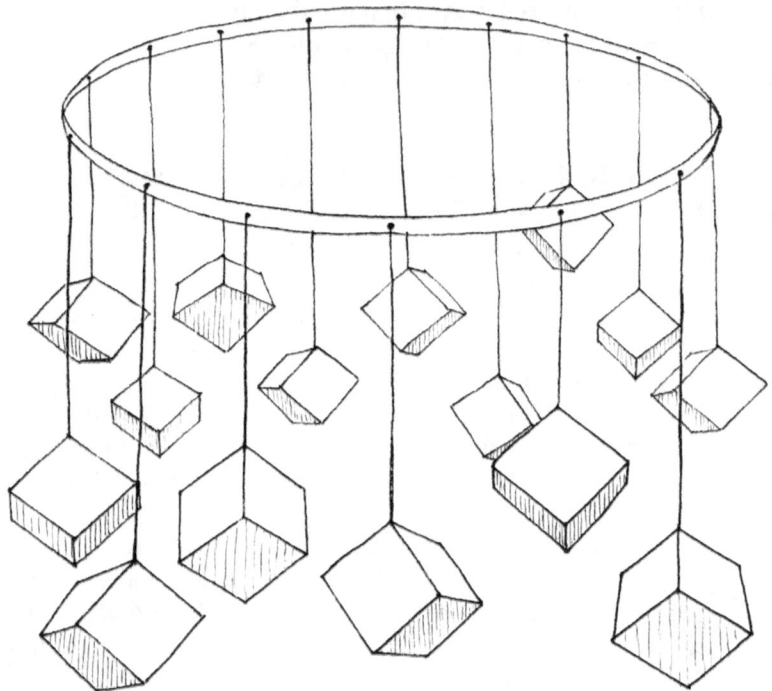

Figure 2.3. "Who am I? Cubes" can be combined to create colorful mobiles to display in the classroom year round, serving as constant reminders of each student's strengths and preferences as an introvert or extrovert. *Kati Haajanen and Esther Aitken.*

conversations. As she states, "The 'Who am I? Cube' often helps students to develop stronger relationships, such as a closer bond with someone who supported them in a game at recess or a new connection with someone who helped them during a group project."[17] (See figure 2.3.)

CHARACTER STRENGTHS: NURTURING QUIET LEADERS

Our introverted students often feel that their dominant style does not qualify as the basis for being a leader in an extrovert-ideal society that prizes charisma, quick decision-making skills, and a passion for speaking in front of crowds. (See table 2.1.) Let's set the record straight by examining the character strengths of quiet leaders.

In 2014, Susan Cain's mission-based company, Quiet Revolution, conducted a study with Dr. John Johnson at Penn State and the Values in Action

Table 2.1. Overview of Introvert/Extrovert Personality Preferences

Personality Preference	Introvert	Extrovert
Social Style	1-1 + Few Close Relationships	Group Work + Meeting New People
Recharging Style	Quiet Times and Spaces	Stimulating Environments (social and/or sensory)
Processing Style	Think to Speak (internal)	Speak to Think (external)

Institute on Character to see whether there might be correlations between personality and character strengths. In 2014, cognitive scientist and humanistic psychologist Dr. Scott Barry Kaufman analyzed the data and found that introversion aligns with three character strengths—humility, perspective, and prudence—strengths that, interestingly, are affiliated with servant leadership.[18] According to the groundbreaking work of Robert Greenleaf, servant leaders believe their organization's goals are best achieved by the development of followers and focus primarily on the growth and well-being of people and the communities to which they belong.[19] The research on leaders who exhibit these strengths helps to dispel myths that characterize introverts as unfit for leadership.

HUMILITY: MISSION-DRIVEN

The results of one large survey found that the appearance and frequency in published books of the words "humility" and "humbleness" dropped, on average, 43 percent between 1901 and 2000.[20] These words often can mean lacking in self-esteem—a sign of weakness—even among our middle-school populations. For instance, a 2016 College of Charleston survey found that 56 percent of fifth and sixth graders said that humble people are "embarrassed, sad, lonely, or shy."[21]

The Values in Action Institute on Character links humility with an accurate assessment of one's strengths and weaknesses, an ability to admit limitations, and a forgetting of the self.[22] In their groundbreaking research on humble leadership, Bradley Owens and David Hekman also found that humble leaders solicit feedback, celebrate team accomplishments over their own, and recognize that they do not have all of the answers. In their 2012 *Journal of Management* study, they went a step further and concluded that humility strengthens a leader's authority because their followers, who know that their input matters, are motivated and emboldened to work harder for the common good.[23]

Just two years after the publication of this study, Google's senior vice president of people relations, Laszlo Bock, deemed humility to be the quality he was looking for in new hires in *Harvard Business Review*'s "The Best Leaders are Humble Leaders." What do humble leaders bring to teams? In this article, he is cited as saying that the most important quality of humble leaders is their ability to make others feel seen and heard, which is directly correlated to innovation.[24]

The energy that can be ignited in organizations with humble leadership is dramatic. Research reveals that humble leaders can create cultures in schools in which teachers are more satisfied with their jobs, students attain higher test scores, and discipline problems decline.[25] Another 2018 study of high-school students found that humble students are more likely to use effective metacognitive strategies and quiz themselves to check their own understanding.[26] He or she might say, "I don't have all the answers. Give me some feedback."

PERSPECTIVE: LISTENING EXPANSIVELY

Imagine two teams with proactive, initiative-taking followers—one team has an introvert as a leader, and the other, an extrovert. Which team is likely to fold the most T-shirts in ten minutes? According to Dr. Adam Grant's lab experiment on the topic, more T-shirts were folded when the leader solicited input from team members. That leader was the introverted listener rather than the extroverted talker (who was unreceptive to followers' ideas). The conclusion? When participants are proactive, teams perform better when led by an introvert rather than an extrovert—28 percent better.[27] And, we can all learn to be better listeners.

Receptivity to others' ideas is at the core of what it means to display perspective. The Values in Action Institute on Character describes the character strength of perspective as the ability to pause and step back to see the big picture and examine the context of any particular situation in order to give "good advice."[28] To give such counsel, the listener must be able to: be fully present with his/her counterpart during a conversation; paraphrase to confirm understanding; and be open to validating emotions in a nonjudgmental way.[29] It's a paradox that we can present to our students: listening makes us more powerful as leaders because we are building trust and enhancing engagement.

An interview with a former introverted high-school exchange student is illuminating when it comes to the introvert "superpower" of perspective. This student, who had a life-changing experience abroad, explains that before she went to Ecuador, she got the advice to be like Mickey Mouse, who has big eyes, big ears, and a very small mouth:

> I think that so much of being an exchange student is learning to understand and really place yourself within the other culture, and let go, as much as possible, of American culture so as to best understand the people around you.[30]

She felt like a "better exchange student" when observing and asking questions before venturing to express her own opinions.

PRUDENCE: THINK BEFORE ACTING

To paraphrase what legendary investor Warren Buffett once said, "When those around you are saying 'Just do it!' be the one to weigh options before making decisions." The chairman and CEO of Berkshire Hathaway asserts that what is needed is the temperament to control the urges that get other people into trouble in investing.[31] This famously introverted investor does not take a "big risk-big reward" approach to risk-taking.

Prudence, the third in the trio of quiet leadership character strengths, is actually unrelated to current notions that associate it with fearfulness. As Arthur C. Brooks notes in "How the Modern World Made Cowards of Us All," "it is only in modern times that we equate prudence with risk aversion."[32] Prudence derives from the Latin "prudentia," meaning sagacity or expertise, and the earliest English usage from the fourteenth century had little to do with risk avoidance. Rather, it signified righteous decision-making rooted in practical wisdom.

Introverts are naturally inclined to weigh options before making a decision or sharing ideas with others, often demonstrating the ability to make innovative connections between disparate concepts. As a leadership expert interviewed for this book said, "When I brought this to light with one particular client, it actually made a huge impact upon him because he could recognize how incredibly smart and in fact brilliant he was, and that there was no relationship between that and his processing speed."[33] (See figure 2.4.)

With this understanding of quiet strengths, we can help our introverted students to self-advocate in personality-diverse communities. Another aspect of our work in nurturing quiet leaders involves providing support so that they can take comfortable risks—or engage in free traits—to attain their own passion-driven goals. We will explore the concept of adaptability and stretching in the next chapter.

30   Chapter 2

Figure 2.4. Introverts prefer to think before they speak, whereas extroverts prefer to speak in order to think. *Kati Haajanen and Esther Aitken.*

REFLECTIONS: MICRO-MINDFUL MOMENTS

"My friend . . . care for your psyche . . . know thyself, for once we know ourselves, we may learn how to care for ourselves."—Socrates

SELF-AWARENESS

1. Do you see yourself as an introvert or extrovert? Why?
2. How might this self-awareness influence your teaching/leading style?

SITUATIONAL AWARENESS

1. Describe a situation that has made you aware of the need for an understanding of the strengths—and challenges—of introverts.

2. Describe a situation where you felt an introvert's temperament was misinterpreted. How did you—or would you now—remedy the situation?

GETTING TO KNOW STUDENTS THROUGH THE TEMPERAMENT LENS

1. Identify three things that both introverted and extroverted students might wish that their teachers understood about their personality style.
2. A "choices" activity for break time is an effective way for you to gain valuable insights into your students' dominant personality styles. With two key questions in mind—"What gives you energy?" and "What saps your energy?"—students can be encouraged to choose an activity that best meets their needs as an introvert or extrovert: reading, sketching, journaling, listening to music, talking with friends, playing a board game, playing a team sport, or assembling a puzzle.

Their answers to these follow-up questions provide valuable insights into their dominant personality style:

- Did you like the activity you chose? Was it an independent activity, or was it shared with a partner or group?
- How did you feel about the space chosen for the activity?
- How did you feel at the end of the activity?

CHARACTER STRENGTHS

> I excel at listening. I realized how powerful this was while attending a weeklong summer camp with girls from my church. The younger campers did all the talking, and when the situation required me to talk, I praised and complimented them. In my own introverted way, this is how I tried to keep a conversation going, but they welcomed the opportunity to have such an eager audience. Not once was I able to walk by without them calling out their nickname for me, smiling and waving. That amount of eager social approval was unusual to me! It took me a while to realize that my ability to listen was what they were responding to. —Quiet Diarist[34]

1. How does this introverted student find her way at summer camp? Have you ever had a similar experience?
2. Can you name colleagues or students who lead through listening?
3. How might you lead strengths-based discussions with your more introverted students?

4. Do you have time for one-on-one conversations with students to build trust and connection (even just for five minutes . . . on a regular basis)? If not, can you advocate for building time into the overall schedule for individual meetings with students?

NURTURING QUIET LEADERS

Based on a strengths-based approach to nurturing quiet leaders, which of the following anecdotal comments resonate the most with you and why?

1. Emily is deliberate in her thoughts/actions and doesn't rush to make judgments.
2. Jeremy forms meaningful relationships and is a sought-after partner in class.
3. Justine is an excellent problem solver who thinks deeply before making a decision.
4. Megan likes to try multiple strategies and is able to persevere in her work.
5. Patrick is an innovative thinker who thrives during independent tasks.
6. Simone reflects deeply and processes her ideas before sharing; she leads by modeling this thoughtful approach to classroom participation.
7. When Adi takes time to speak slowly and offer thoughtful reflections, he empowers other students to do the same.
8. Inez is very attentive to details, which serves her well in long-term projects.

Chapter 3

Adaptability and Stretching

"In a gentle way, you can shake the world."—Mahatma Gandhi

We are all more than our innate introverted/extroverted personality traits. We have free will that enables us to make choices that are not bound by our biogenetic nature. This ability to step outside our comfort zone is what gives us the flexibility to act in ways that may not align perfectly with our inborn nature. For example, an introverted student can be the first to speak up during a team meeting, and an extroverted student can listen deeply to others during a classroom discussion. The challenge is to flex our styles in ways that do not lead to either burnout or self-negation.

ADAPTABILITY, FREE TRAITS, AND CORE PERSONAL PROJECTS

Adaptability is a personality trait just like introversion and extroversion. This trait comprises approximately 40 percent of our identity, according to Dr. Adam Grant, best-selling author of six books and professor of organizational psychology at the University of Pennsylvania's Wharton School. In his WorkLife podcast, Grant's guest, Dr. Brian Little, distinguished research professor emeritus at Carleton and director of the Social Ecology Research Group (SERG) at Cambridge, posits that "free traits"—or tendencies expressed by individual choice—coexist with inborn fixed traits (see chapter 2) in our complex selves.[1]

According to Dr. Little, it is our dedication to a "core personal project," or meaningful and manageable personal goal, that often drives us to engage in "free traits."[2] When stretching in the service of our own passions and interests, and not in the service of societal expectations of what it means to be "successful"—which is often related to money, status, and prestige—such flexing brings us joy. For instance, when an introverted graduate student is so passionate about the French language that she wants to share it with others—and become a teacher—she can learn to speak dynamically in front of groups even though it is not part of her innate personality to do so.

In his 2017 article, "How Our Projects Shape Our Personalities—and How We Can Use Them to Remake Who We Are," Little affirms that we pursue many different kinds of core personal projects in our lives, ranging from "grandiose" occupational ones to "simple" recreational ones.[3] The following is a list of Little's six categories of core personal projects, with an example for each. While the examples are designed for educators, they can be modified easily for students:

- Occupational Project: Give a presentation at a national educational conference.
- Interpersonal Project: Have coffee with members of a different department.
- Maintenance Project: Spend time on Saturday afternoons in the library reading books on wellness.
- Recreational Project: Take a pickleball class.
- Health/Body Project: Join a fitness club with a monthly membership.
- Intrapersonal Project: Manage negative self-talk before and after parent–teacher conferences.

When engaging in conversations with students about their core personal projects, we need to remind them that such goals should be both meaningful *and* manageable. For example, if a high-school boy broke his ankle on the lacrosse field in April, it might not be manageable for him to lead a hiking trip for middle schoolers in May. A 1985 study by Janet Polivy and Peter Herman of the University of Toronto notes that planning for unmanageable goals can result in "false hope syndrome."[4] We should advise our students to set goals that are grounded in a realistic assessment of both the time needed to plan for and execute the goal and the resources needed to attain this goal.

Dr. Little's research suggests that whether the core personal project is seemingly imposing or insignificant, the following questions should be applied as we help our students think through and plan for a new or unfamiliar task:

- Is this goal both worthwhile and attainable?
- Why is it important to follow through with the goal?
- Who does the goal benefit?
- How might you grow in the process?

Adaptability and Stretching

STRETCH METER STRATEGY

It is critical to emphasize that overriding our inborn nature for extended amounts of time, and in ways that are too draining, can lead to a harmful outcome: self-negation, or trying to be someone we are not. The challenge is to stretch in ways that still honor our inborn introverted or extroverted nature. How can we do this? As Susan Cain writes in *Quiet*, thinking of the self as a rubber band is immensely helpful: we can flex when we want to, but if pulled too far, we will snap.[5] Self-awareness about what gives us energy—and what saps our energy—is critical (see chapter 2).

Identifying the intensity of a stretch on a scale of one to ten, with the one-to-three range as something that comes naturally, the four-to-six range as something that is relatively uncomfortable, and the seven-to-ten range as something that is potentially stressful, is immensely helpful in guiding students through the process of planning ahead. (See figure 3.1.) For instance, if an introverted student is accustomed to staying home reading on Friday nights, rather than going out with friends, she may want to try to stretch

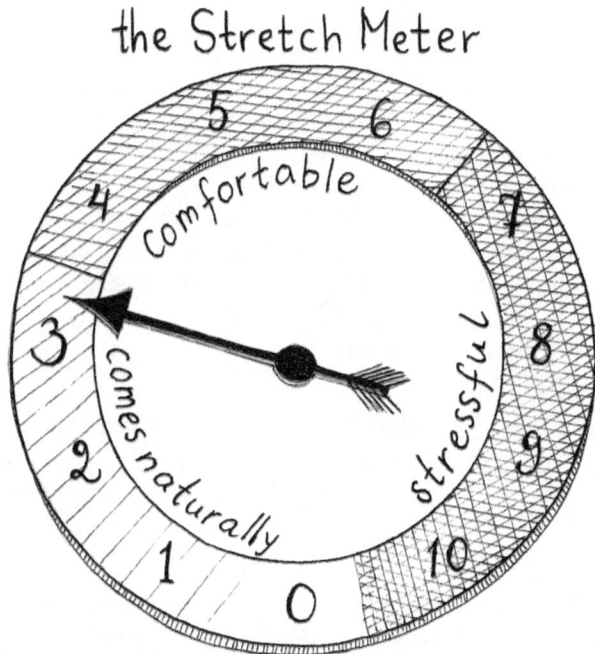

Figure 3.1. The Stretch Meter strategy helps introverts and extroverts alike to identify goals that are challenging, but not so challenging that they might snap when they stretch. *Kati Haajanen and Esther Aitken.*

herself by attending a birthday party. However, this same student may not be ready—yet—to give a speech to the entire grade. An extroverted student might need to gauge whether it is too stressful to stay at home on a Saturday night to work alone on a project rather than attend a weekly Saturday evening movie club.

The aim is to have our students feel challenged as they strive to realize their goals but not so challenged that they either freeze up or give up on the project. This can be done with the aid of a Stretch Meter, which encourages students to take the time needed to think through the comfort level of any given core personal project. (See tables 3.1 and 3.2.) It is a useful tool for conversations with students about their temperament type, the levels of stress affiliated with any given project, and ways to achieve their goals. If the goal is potentially stressful, it is important to know that this is the case before embarking on what might be a long and arduous journey.

Using a Stretch Meter helps all students determine their comfort level in flexing their styles, and in particular, enables the introvert to plan ahead to obtain a realistic perspective of how much energy will be required to attain a certain goal.[6]

Scaffolding a "Dining Hall Stretch" for Introverted Students

Let's focus on a common experience of introverts in the bustling dining hall, a place that is notorious for being overwhelming and overstimulating for introverts. The author recalls that she used to shun the cafeteria at college if she didn't set plans in advance with her small group of friends; rather than eating alone or attempting to meet strangers in the cafeteria, she stayed in her room and dined on snack food. Oftentimes, her reaction to the dining hall was such that the "fight, flight or freeze" side of her nervous system—the sympathetic

Table 3.1. Stretch Meter for Introverts

	Comes Naturally (1–3)	Relatively Comfortable (4–6)	Potentially Stressful (7–10)
Core Personal Project	Reading a book alone under a tree	Attending a family birthday dessert party	Attending a friend's basketball tournament
Ways to Prepare & Achieve Goal	Find a favorite genre book to read	Talk with cousins in advance and plan to hang out together	Connect with other friends who are going to the event and sit together. By showing up, you acknowledge the importance of this event for your friend

Table 3.2. Stretch Meter for Extroverts

	Comes Naturally (1–3)	Relatively Comfortable (4–6)	Potentially Stressful (7–10)
Core Personal Project	Attending a school pep rally	Listening to classmates before raising my hand to speak aloud	Working independently on a class project
Ways to Prepare & Achieve Goal	Find out when the next rally will take place	Jot down three responses before raising my hand	Contact experts in the field to interview for the project. Offer to share the project at a school event

side—propelled her to simply exit, rather than introducing herself to others and socializing during the meal. So, without calculated stretching, she simply shut down and stayed home.

One of the elementary school educators interviewed for this book describes how the overstimulating cafeteria environment can make it difficult for introverted students to make quick food choices:

> Part of the challenge is that you just have a lot of people in one space. Our dining room is overwhelming for a lot of reasons . . . the walls are all white and very bright with kind of stark lighting. You also have too many choices . . . It's a great problem to have, but you have so many different options of what you can eat. And then you've got one hundred and fifty little girls and they're trying to figure out what they're going to eat, plus teachers, so the noise level is high.[7]

The same educator intervenes to help introverted children find their place in the crowd, starting with food choices: (See figure 3.2.)

> I watch some of them just kind of walk aimlessly with these big eyes . . . when we notice kids doing that, we try to walk around with them and say things such as, 'Oh, do you like watermelon?' I try to help them make some choices so they can sit down and actually eat a meal instead of just being paralyzed with uncertainty and too much choice.

She continues, "I love this idea of simply cutting back on choice, promoting the well-being of those students who are more prone to overthinking decisions, and particularly when you have that light and that noise."[8] In this way, educators can help prudent decision-makers take action when time pressure does not allow for enough "time to think."

Figure 3.2. A quiet-friendly cafeteria is one that allows space for introverts to find their place in the crowd. *Kati Haajanen and Esther Aitken.*

SCAFFOLDING A "PUBLIC SPEAKING STRETCH" FOR INTROVERTED STUDENTS

Imagine a student who is passionate about establishing a new club that will publish a yearly current-events magazine, but who is fearful of making a pitch to the entire grade is mandatory for starting any club. What advice will be most helpful to this aspiring introverted leader, who is motivated by a passion for opening up a space for dialogue about current affairs?

In coaching any quiet student who is planning for this sort of "stressful" stretch, it is imperative that there be time in advance for practicing and gathering feedback from a trusted friend, family member, or teacher. First, begin with these questions: Why does it matter to our community that we have a current-affairs magazine? How is your passion connected to the larger purpose of the community? Counsel the student to conduct empathy interviews to get to know more about how their own passion connects with the needs of the student body and gather feedback to refine the idea and connect it with the realities of school life, including resource management. Is there a budget for this initiative? Will there be faculty advisors? What about an editorial staff?

Once there is conviction around the purpose, invite this quiet leader to write the required speech, making sure it is concise yet conveys the deeper meaning of the initiative. Enhancing any mission statement with personal stories, rather than simply listing facts and figures, will help ensure that the message is delivered in such a way as to inspire others to join the club.

Before the speech, advise the student to visit the presentation space, practice multiple times, and pay attention to the congruence among speech, tone, and body language. As an introverted high-school student advises,

> Ask someone to proofread your speech for you, practice with the acting teacher, practice it until it just feels natural and it feels comfortable. If you're giving the speech from your heart, it will be easier than you think to give the speech because you care about it.[9]

This high-school senior's comments about a message "coming from the heart" are well supported by public speaking experts around the globe. When we speak about our passions, what deeply stirs us, we naturally will be more enthusiastic, emitting the positive energy needed to connect with the audience in a meaningful way. (See figure 3.3.) Advise students to make eye contact with those in the audience who appear to be engaged rather than distracted or bored. During her senior year, in front of two thousand people, this student "got through" her presentation—with great success—by connecting in the moment with familiar faces in the audience: "I guess I knew a lot of people in the audience so I'd think, 'That's my friend, so I'm making eye contact with them. That's the kid that I had in the afterschool program, so, this is fine.'"[10]

Regardless of whether the initiative comes to fruition or the idea for a new club becomes a reality, the most important outcome for the student involves the growth that occurs from taking a calculated risk to manifest their idea. Such growth will never occur if the student withholds information or engages in self-silencing due to a fear of public speaking. There is always the chance to learn from mistakes and apply that knowledge when trying again in the

Figure 3.3. Coaching introverted students in public speaking involves three important elements: helping them to focus on their passion and mission, encouraging them to practice their speech in front of different audiences, and supporting them as they visit the presentation space in advance of the event. *Kati Haajanen and Esther Aitken.*

future. It may be that the student needs to recalibrate the goal itself so that passion and purpose are aligned.

A "FREE TRAIT AGREEMENT" APPROACH FOR EDUCATORS

When coaching our students about stepping outside of their comfort zones in the name of a core personal project, it is immensely helpful to practice what Dr. Brian Little refers to as the "Free Trait Agreement" with our own colleagues, friends, and partners. Such a compromise requires us to meet each other halfway when it comes to activities that can energize or drain us.[11] It helps us to set the stage for our students as they strive to remain true to themselves as they step outside their comfort zones.

A Free Trait Agreement with another adult in our lives acknowledges that at times, we each need to flex our styles—in exchange for being allowed to be ourselves the rest of the time. For example, when an extroverted principal decrees that all educators need to attend the weekly Friday social gathering, which is often too draining for an introverted teacher after a long week in the classroom, a Free Trait Agreement is reached when both the principal and the introverted educator agree that the teacher will attend one social gathering per month.

On a more personal basis, a Free Trait Agreement may be created when an extroverted partner wants to go out every Saturday for a full day of social activities, and her introverted partner voices a need for quiet recharging time on Saturdays. The compromise? A Free Trait Agreement might allow for a full day of social activities on the first Saturday of the month.

This sort of agreement is a testament to the fact that stretching and recharging go hand in hand. The need for solitude is explored in depth in chapter 7, "Rescuing Solitude," and a myriad of ways to create quiet spaces in classrooms, cafeterias, faculty rooms, and on school grounds is the topic of chapter 8, "Quiet Spaces."

REFLECTIONS: MICRO-MINDFUL MOMENTS

"I have to be alone very often. I'd be quite happy if I spent from Saturday night until Monday morning alone in my apartment. That's how I refuel."—Audrey Hepburn

IDENTIFYING CORE PERSONAL PROJECTS

1. What kinds of activities excite you?
2. What kinds of activities sap your energy?

FLEXING YOUR STYLE: SUCCESSES

1. Can you think of a time when you experienced success while stretching outside of your comfort zone?
2. What was it about this goal that made you want to move outside your comfort zone?
3. How challenging was it for you to do so?

FLEXING YOUR STYLE: CHALLENGES

1. Have you ever flexed too far—and "snapped" like a rubber band? If so, when? Were you trying to fulfill someone's expectations of what it means to be "successful?" Explain.
2. What might you do differently next time? How can you remain true to your temperament while striving to attain a stretch goal?

SCAFFOLDING A "SPEAKING UP FIRST STRETCH" FOR STUDENTS

If I'm working with adults, or a smaller group of student leaders, then I'll call on people out of the natural order. So, the natural order would be the extroverts first. And so what I'll do is call on the quieter members, not necessarily all of them and not in a way that's rude, but I might call on some of the quieter people first. I want to stretch their rubber bands so they get to experience how they might be able to move the conversation with their words and even open up the conversation.—Leadership Educator[12]

1. If you know that one of your introverted students does not want to speak up first in a class, do you think that it is ever appropriate to call on them first? Why or why not?
2. How can you scaffold this stretch, with patience and empathy, so that it is not overly stressful?
3. What steps can you take with quieter students before class so that they are able to "stretch their rubber bands" and experience how they might be able to move the conversation forward by speaking up first?

"FREE TRAIT AGREEMENT"

1. Why might this type of agreement be a useful tool for honoring both yourself and others in life's daily, weekly, or monthly situations?
2. Do you see any downsides to this type of agreement?
3. Provide an example of a situation where you would feel comfortable making a Free Trait Agreement with a colleague, friend, or partner.

Section II

CREATING INTROVERT-FRIENDLY CLASSROOMS

Chapter 4

From Participation to Engagement

"Quiet people have the loudest minds."—Stephen Hawking

TEACHING IS A DANCE

Teaching is akin to a waltz: the smoothest of dance routines appears simple but actually involves a complicated series of choreographed steps. Teaching takes hours of rehearsal time and a willingness to pivot as needed in the moment. When it looks easy, you know the educator is practicing their role with expertise. A subtle combination of lesson planning and improvisation enables all learners, introverted and extroverted alike, to feel empowered to be wholly present, take risks, and authentically connect with the material.

One dance move that can be highly effective in setting the stage for creating an introvert-friendly classroom involves freezing time during an extrovert-dominated discussion by hitting "pause" on the lesson plan. The educator can invite everyone in the room to raise their hand—in silence—and take a look around them. (See figure 4.1.) Then, in a light-hearted way, the educator can elicit commentary about the distinct styles of hand-raising in the classroom: Why does Amanda simply lift her hand droopily, cradling her elbow in her hand? What about Sean, who shoots his hand up straight in the air with his palm extended? And Kimberly, who extends two fingers to the right, as if gesturing for the check after enjoying a meal with friends? Often, this exercise elicits laughter, and some students might exclaim, "This is a strange thing to do!"

Possibilities for substituting the traditional practice of classroom participation, or calling on students who raise their hands first, with a more expansive approach to classroom engagement are forged in the crucible of such student

Figure 4.1. Deconstructing the traditional class participation paradigm begins with students' self-awareness about their own tendencies for raising their hands in the classroom. *Kati Haajanen and Esther Aitken.*

self-realization. When our students are ready to try something new, the teacher has the buy-in to experiment with the tango rather than the waltz. One of these new "dance moves" involves valuing silence and solitude as vital forms of human connection and creativity.

Opportunities for experimenting with new pedagogical approaches are also rooted in the self-awareness of educators themselves. Witness a teacher's self-reflection about both playing to her strengths and stepping outside of her comfort zone while leading classroom discussions:

> As an introverted teacher, sometimes I actually lean a little bit more on my students to do the talking. I love sitting back, observing, watching them work in their process. But I also realize that I need to shape and guide that . . . so I prepare things in advance so that my students can see and hear information in multiple ways.[1]

This educator adds that as a student herself, she never liked the idea of being assessed on what she verbally contributed to classroom conversations: "It was challenging for me to follow the threads of what everyone was saying, absorb, come up with my own thoughts, and find the right time to share them."[2] In her own classroom, she is keenly aware of the need to set the stage for both verbal and non-verbal contributions by embracing a broader, more temperament-inclusive notion of what it means to participate in class.

Another self-aware educator, an English teacher from the Midwest, recalls that as a child, she was exceedingly engaged in class. Nevertheless, she suffered from anxiety when trying to fit into the mold of an ideal classroom participant for whom quantity of speech mattered more than quality of speech. As she recalls, "I had pre-participation anxiety, and then I would talk, and then had post-participation anxiety." After two decades of teaching, this educator can easily spot students who are inclined to think before they speak: those who are energized by silence and yet still actively engaged in the class. As she states, "I can see it in their eyeballs, I can see it in their body language, and I can see it in their writing that they are super engaged."[3]

STRIKING A BALANCE BETWEEN SILENCE AND TALK

A temperament-inclusive classroom is characterized by a balance between independent work and collaborative learning and between solitude and group work. Such a classroom rewards quality of speech over quantity and deep listening and writing as varied forms of classroom engagement. By embracing this broader structure of classroom engagement, we can begin to create opportunities for students to engage with classmates through both silence and speech.

The goal is to shift traditional practices to value silence, as well as speech, rather than assuming that silence connotes one or more of the following: compliance, insecurity, resistance, or boredom. As we create opportunities for both solitude and teamwork in our classrooms, we honor the learning style of approximately one-third to one-half of our students, who are likely to fall on the introverted side of the introvert–extrovert spectrum.

When shifting cultural norms around solitude in the classroom—in the form of short, reflective pauses or longer periods of independent work—it is important for an educator to discern the difference between the energizing silence of the engaged participant and the silencing that may be the product of complex racial, gender, and/or cultural dynamics. Once we can identify constructive nonverbal engagement, we can help all of our students to refine their active listening skills, adjust their body language postures, and reach out through written forms of communication.

NONVERBAL ENGAGEMENT: ACTIVE LISTENING

In the quest to shift our definition of classroom participation from quantity of speech to quality of speech, and from one mode of communication to multiple channels of engagement, it is critical not only to recognize the listeners in our classes but also to teach them how to be better listeners.

What constitutes good listening? According to Jack Zenger and Joseph Folkman in "What Great Listeners Actually Do," active listening involves the creation of a safe space in which ideas can be shared, feedback flows smoothly, and counterparts feel seen, valued, and heard. The listener begins by seeking to understand the main idea of what the other person is saying by asking questions and restating issues to confirm their understanding. As their interaction continues, the listener increasingly understands their counterpart's perspective.[4] The goal? To actively acknowledge the other's feelings in a supportive, nonjudgmental way. Overall, good listening is not passive at all; it involves taking a vigorous interest in what is being communicated.

Teaching these listening skills is an integral way to cultivate empathy in our students. The paradox of active listening is that by appearing to relinquish power, we actually become more powerful. As Amy Cuddy states in *Presence,* listening builds trust, enables us to acquire useful information and see others as potential allies, and allows us to develop solutions together since everyone feels as though they have been heard.[5]

A significant part of silent communication involves nonverbal cues, such as facial expressions, respiration rates, gestures, postures, and numerous other subtle body-language signals. (See figure 4.2.) It is estimated that 80 percent of what we communicate comes from these signals. Research shows that people decide how competent we are in a fraction of a second, and the most important indicator is body language. In her "Power and Influence" video, Stanford Business Professor Deborah Gruenfeld cautions us to pay more attention to body language than speech, as it communicates both power and status. As she says, competence is based 7 percent on words, 38 percent on presentation, and 55 percent on body language.[6]

Figure 4.2. We can help our students to demonstrate that they are engaged in active listening by teaching body language skills, including facial expressions. *Kati Haajanen and Esther Aitken.*

We can help students demonstrate that they are engaged in active listening by teaching body language skills, including facial expressions and upper body movements. As professional speaker Patti Wood states, turning toward the person who is speaking *with our hearts* indicates that we care about what the speaker is saying.[7] In this process, it's important to note that introverts, who tend to excel at listening, often struggle with eye contact while talking but give solid eye contact while listening. Extroverts, on the other hand, often make solid eye contact while talking but tend to look around when listening.[8]

Here are some tips for helping students adopt more confident and inviting body language:

- Give facial feedback: React to what the speaker is saying, so that they know you are listening, by gently nodding your head or smiling when appropriate.
- Make eye contact: Facial muscles should be relaxed so that eye contact does not come across as an intense or intimidating stare.
- Lean forward to show you are interested. Leaning back indicates dominance.
- Turn the upper body toward the speaker. There is no need to *directly* face the speaker if the seating arrangement does not allow it.

When students demonstrate active listening, educators can celebrate this form of engagement with anecdotal comments that let students know that they are being seen and valued as listeners. The following Active Listening Rubric is designed to help teachers recognize and record this type of classroom involvement. (See table 4.1.) This is just one of four rubrics in this chapter that can be used for a specific class or project or as a running record throughout the year with dates and notes recorded in the boxes.[9]

Table 4.1. Active Listening Rubric

	Rarely	*Sometimes*	*Frequently*
Makes eye contact with the speaker			
Gives facial feedback to the speaker (Smiling, Nodding)			
Avoids distractions			
Moves body toward the speaker			
Seeks to understand the speaker by restating ideas or asking questions			

Chapter 4

NONVERBAL ENGAGEMENT: WRITTEN REFLECTIONS

Introverted students are often inclined to demonstrate their engagement through notes, emails, online chats, and digital forums. It's incumbent upon the educator to invite written dialogue before, during, and after class. As with sensitivity to other forms of nonverbal engagement, developing this approach is rooted in self-awareness. As one educator says, "I think that one of my biggest strengths is my ability to break down complex concepts and lead students through a discovery process in a very systematic way." As someone who teaches through inquiry, her goal is to pique students' curiosity about the topic first, and then step back and let them do the discovery. Next, she quietly supports them through the written word: "I like to do little notes on their science notebooks if they need them. With older students, I will often send them an email. With all students, I will write them little notes and leave them on their desks."[10]

Another educator from the East Coast concurs about "little notes." She endeavors to teach her students that sharing thoughts can be powerful in both verbal and nonverbal formats. She says, "There are always little slips of paper everywhere available for them to jot things down. And they can either give them to me or not, but it doesn't have to be that they have to share at that moment."[11] Her goal is to try to honor equally both listeners and talkers.

Figure 4.3. After contributing an insightful comment to a class discussion, introverts often prefer a written form of validation to a public display of recognition. *Kati Haajanen and Esther Aitken.*

Table 4.2. Written Reflections Rubric

	Rarely	Sometimes	Frequently
Shows depth of understanding			
Makes connections			
Develops original ideas			
Demonstrates curiosity			
Demonstrates growth mindset			
Asks insightful questions			

As a middle school English teacher says, (See figure 4.3) public validation can sometimes be counterproductive for our introverted students, so a written form can be the best way to acknowledge an insightful contribution from an introverted student: "So, I'll email them to say, 'The connection that you made between this character and that painting that we looked at was really outstanding.'"[12]

Reaching out on a one-on-one basis is powerful. Some of the best conversations educators have with introverted students occur over Google Docs (or a similar platform) when they go back and forth with ideas and comments. Introverted students often crave that form of written connection with their teacher. The Written Reflections Rubric helps educators to assess this modality of classroom engagement. (See table 4.2.)

VERBAL ENGAGEMENT

Cold calling is the nemesis of introverts. As a head of school in the Northeast admits, "I was pretty quiet. I used to hate cold calling in school. It used to terrify me. So, you're just a sitting duck and oh, did I hate that. And I just never want anyone else that I teach to feel the way that I did. That's not a good learning environment, I think. It wasn't for me."[13]

When it comes to verbal engagement, educators can opt for an inclusive strategy that invites all students to participate at least once during a full classroom discussion. Many educators interviewed for this book use popsicle sticks—with the students' names on them—as a way to level the playing field for introverts and extroverts alike. Instead of raising hands, an educator can randomly pull out a popsicle stick and then let that student know that they can either speak or pass when their name is pulled from the "bouquet." Educators can always return to students who choose not to answer in the first round.

Table 4.3. Verbal Engagement Rubric: Large/Small Group

	Rarely	Sometimes	Frequently
Participates at the beginning of the conversation			
Sums up ideas at the end of the conversation			
Offers original ideas and opposing viewpoints			
Extends discussion by building on the ideas of others			
Invites others into the conversation			
Asks relevant questions			
Reads passages aloud from a text			

Moreover, varied forms of verbal participation in the classroom—full classroom discussions, small group interactions, dialogues in pairs—provide students with an array of opportunities to share ideas verbally with the rest of the group. The Verbal Engagement Rubric: Large/Small Group is designed to help educators to give feedback about their behaviors in large and small group discussions. (See table 4.3.)

With the dance improv metaphor in mind, educators can adopt a flexible approach to collaborative work by noticing when it's time to move from a large group discussion to a small group one, and then on to duos. As a seasoned teacher states, "My goal is to get my whole class of students to engage in an academic conversation where they're all equal participants in building on one another's thoughts, challenging each other, asking questions."[14] Setting boundaries for the more naturally loquacious students is critical: ask these students to imagine three class participation tokens. When these three tokens have been used up, it's time to listen. Note that the same strategy can work for introverts, too: they have three tokens for verbal participation, and once they have been used up, it's time to ease back into listening.

Conversations in pairs often set the stage for greater ease of verbal participation in a larger group discussion (see chapter 5 for Think-Pair-Share partnerships). The catch is to know when to shift from one verbal modality to another. As an introvert-inclusive educator exclaims,

> I watch and can see a student trying to break into the conversation who doesn't know how to negotiate that. And then I pause the conversation by saying, "I want you to turn to the person next to you now and discuss this small thing." So, I'll break my larger group into just a series of small partner talks. Sometimes just narrowing the audience can help an introvert.[15]

Table 4.4. Verbal Engagement Rubric: Duos

	Rarely	Sometimes	Frequently
Demonstrates interest in working with any partner (in addition to a close friend)			
Tries to understand the partner's perspective on an issue			
Builds on the ideas of the partner			
Takes turns with the partner when sharing out to the larger group			

The Verbal Engagement Rubric: Duos places an emphasis on the way that each member of the duo tries to understand the other's perspective. (See table 4.4.)

It is important to emphasize that the rubrics in this chapter are designed to help educators both keep track of students' engagement in a variety of modalities and assess these varied forms of student engagement. They can thus help educators notice when and if they are relying too heavily on the traditional class participation model, whereby the first hand "in the air" gets "air time." With this sort of self-awareness, educators can foster quiet-friendly cultures, ensuring that there is "space" in their classrooms for those who prefer talking *and* those who prefer listening. In doing so, they can help introverted and extroverted students alike to own their strengths *and* step outside their comfort zones.

In the next chapter, we explore three approaches to setting the stage for verbal participation: the Long Runway, reflective pausing, and brainwriting, as well as ways to celebrate silence as a prelude to talk in anecdotal comments.

REFLECTIONS: MICRO-MINDFUL MOMENTS

"Without great solitude no serious work is possible."—Pablo Picasso

THE EXPECTATION TO "JUST SPEAK UP"

We, as a society, have constructed that the way you show your engagement is by talking, raising your hands, reading out loud. There are so many other ways to show engagement, with eye contact, body language, individual conversations, and writing in notebooks. And I use all of those in my room. But I know that there are still a lot of teachers, even at our school, and especially with older grades, who really fall back on that, "Well, she doesn't talk enough in class" kind of model. And I think that the constant pressure to speak up and raise your hands . . . period after period, day after day, can be really draining for kids.—Lower School Educator[16]

1. What does this comment reveal about common attitudes in our schools toward classroom participation? Does this comment pertain to your school or organization?
2. Based on the information in chapter 2 about temperament diversity, how might you explain the biological basis for feeling drained when pressured to "speak up"? How might you tailor your explanation to the age level that you teach?

FROM PARTICIPATION TO ENGAGEMENT

1. Have you ever (even unwittingly) criticized a student, or seen a colleague criticize a student, for being quiet in class?
2. How is class participation defined in your school?
3. What are some of the different ways that students express both engagement and disengagement in your classes?

STRIKING A BALANCE BETWEEN SILENCE AND TALK

1. What is the relationship between talk and silence in your classroom? How can talk and silence be seen along a continuum?
2. What are some possible reasons for student silence? When should a teacher investigate student silence and when should they support it?
3. How can you encourage colleagues to value nonverbal behaviors as much as verbal ones as a way to promote temperament inclusivity?

ACTIVE LISTENING

1. How much do you currently value active listening as a classroom engagement skill?
2. What are some of the challenges that you face in teaching active listening skills (such as eye contact) to your students?

3. How can you best assess your students' ability to listen as a classroom engagement skill? How can the Active Listening Rubric be a useful tool to recognize and record student behaviors and help you to become more aware of your own pedagogy?

WRITTEN REFLECTIONS

1. How can you leverage the written word to develop quiet-friendly classrooms?
2. Among all of the ways to assess writing in the Written Reflections Rubric, which one resonates the most with you and why?
3. Do you have a regular practice of using an "exit ticket" (which asks students about their takeaways from any given lesson) to assess the effectiveness of a lesson? If so, can you think of an example that helped you better connect with an individual learner?

LARGE/SMALL GROUP DISCUSSIONS

"In the classroom, I see myself as a conductor charged with calibrating and distributing verbal and nonverbal contributions."—Leadership Educator[17]

1. Does the conductor metaphor resonate with you? If so, why? If not, why not?
2. What are some techniques that you employ to create a sense of belonging for all students in your classes?

CONVERSATIONS IN PAIRS/DUOS

1. How often do you ask students to turn and talk to their neighbor?
2. Do you find that this strategy helps to make students comfortable with a full group discussion? If so, provide an example of a particularly fruitful "pairs conversation."

Chapter 5

Silence as Prelude to Talk

"We had to conceive of silence in order to open our ears."—John Cage

The phrase "Be quiet!" is deeply ingrained in our school cultures as a quasi-punitive measure spoken in the name of classroom management. The author still vividly remembers repeated moments when she was in the fifth grade, and her entire class was constantly admonished to "Be quiet! Put your head on your desk!" The instructor's tone indicated anger and frustration at all students, despite the fact that those who had provoked her reaction were often the same small group of loud and unruly kids.

When "quiet" is used in a disciplinary manner, introverted students, in particular, are prone to feelings of shame and inferiority. Introverts are naturally inclined to think before they speak, taking time to process thoughts internally before sharing them with others. This style is the opposite of that of extroverts, who are inclined to speak in order to think. The introverted inclination to reflect quietly before sharing an idea or making a decision constitutes a communication and problem-solving style that we need to nurture in our classrooms.

By creating quiet times in our classrooms—in a non-punitive manner—we help *both* introverted and extroverted students build self-awareness, deepen knowledge, and make connections. We can normalize silence in our classrooms with three techniques: the Long Runway, reflective pausing, and brainwriting. These approaches can serve as the basis for writing quiet-friendly anecdotal comments, which recognize both a student's silence (reflection and listening) and talk (in pairs, small groups, or large groups). The sample comments at the end of this chapter are designed to guide educators in writing comments that honor "silent talk."

LONG RUNWAY

The Long Runway approach is rooted in the fact that it often takes an introvert more time than an extrovert to acclimate to a new situation or environment. Planning ahead to meet this need allows introverts to participate more fully in classroom activities.[1] The Long Runway also gives extroverts time to filter through their ideas and bring more focus to any activity.

Providing agendas and essential questions in advance (twenty-four hours, if possible) is an effective way to provide students with a Long Runway. (See figure 5.1.) We can even ask the students themselves to help us display agendas, daily schedules, or essential questions at the beginning of the school day (depending on their age and the school schedule); this important part of planning ahead becomes a communal task, with student ownership of this process. We also can ask students for their written takeaways at the end of class so that their feedback is incorporated into our agenda for the next day's lesson: "What worked for you? What didn't work for you?" In this way, student voices can be quietly incorporated into the plan for the next lesson.

Providing a Long Runway begins before class and continues the *instant* a teacher walks into the classroom. Within a few minutes, an educator can survey the room, watching for student expressions that convey a variety of emotions, from joy to boredom, enthusiasm to anger, and motivation to anxiety. Depending on the class size and age of students, educators can allow a couple of minutes of check-in time for students to air their feelings about an upcoming school event or converse with a buddy about last night's reading assignment. During this crucial yet unstructured time, teachers can also connect nonverbally with kids in the room: a quick nod, thumbs-up or thumbs-down gesture, a smile. Silence and talk can coexist during this check-in period.

A lower school teacher interviewed for the book suggests an approach to this sort of check-in that levels the "talking field" for younger students. She states,

Figure 5.1. The Long Runway approach, which involves providing agendas and questions in advance, gives introverts the time they need to prepare for classroom activities so that they can fully engage in the moment. *Kati Haajanen and Esther Aitken.*

For the elementary kids, we sit in a circle and first think about how they are feeling, and then I pass around some object, such as a puppet or animal—a different one each day. And whoever is holding the object has a turn, if they so desire, to share how they are feeling.[2]

The combination of the security engendered by holding something "fuzzy and cute" with the directive that they can animate that object helps everyone to become calm and focused.

To counteract the busy, overstimulating environment in schools today, a middle school library director helps her students to "drop into the present" by starting classes with a mindful bell:

For about a minute and a half to two minutes, I ring a bell that has different notes. And when I start the process, I just say to students we need to get grounded in the moment. I don't give them any instructions except for the fact that they have to be quiet during that time.[3]

Over time, this skilled educator offers more explicit directions to her students during silent check-in time: "I invite them to pay attention to their breath by noticing the rise and fall of their belly, the cold air coming in through their nose and mouth, and the warm air leaving." She then asks them to pay attention to the sensations of their body: noticing their feet on the ground, the air on their skin, and their back on the chair. Finally, students are invited to pay attention to the sounds they hear while sitting together in silence, paying particular attention to just one thing.[4] Such a mindful practice helps both educators and students to switch gears from one class to the next so they are ready to teach and learn together.

With such unstructured time in a quiet, mindful, and judgment-free zone, students are able to figuratively enter or re-enter the learning space with a refreshed sense of openness and trust. These few still moments can pave the way for increased concentration and engagement throughout the lesson.

REFLECTIVE PAUSING

Embedding opportunities for silent reflection during class enables introverts and extroverts alike to build self-awareness, enhance motivation, deepen knowledge, and spark imagination. Taking time to think helps students better understand what they have learned, identify areas of struggle, and make connections with other disciplines—and with the real world. These connections are potentially the catalyst for the birth of innovative solutions to problems. As one teacher reported, during such reflective pausing, a high-school student may just dream up a way to connect the arts and sciences in the quest to alleviate the suffering of Alzheimer's patients! One of our ultimate goals as educators is to cultivate in our students the ability to find and solve real-world problems and concerns. Providing students with time to access prior knowledge and absorb content is essential in this regard.

It is commonplace for teachers to pause for just *one second* between asking a question and calling upon a student. The quick auditory processors—the extroverts—are at an advantage in this situation. Without slowing down the time they take before calling upon a student, teachers may leave some students, especially the introverted ones, behind. As Patricia Jennings explains in *Mindfulness for Teachers: Simple Skill for Peace and Productivity in the Classroom*, educational researchers have shown that students are in a better position to respond with greater complexity and accuracy when the teacher pauses for as long as three to five seconds after posing a question. Over time, the effects can be dramatic: many students show an increased level of engagement and higher achievement test scores. In addition, school retention levels increase.[5] (See figure 5.2.)

Figure 5.2. "Wait time" enables introverts, who need processing time, to be included in a classroom discussion. *Kati Haajanen and Esther Aitken*.

Table 5.1. Benefits of Think Time

Time to Think	Benefits of Reflective Pausing for Students
5 to 10 seconds of quiet reflection before calling on students	To offer more complex answers to questions
1 to 3 minutes for Micro-Mindful Moments (as per the last section of each chapter of this book)	To make connections between personal experiences and a topic and to consider multiple perspectives before coming to conclusions
3 to 5 minutes for the observation of an idea, formula, or object	To question underlying assumptions and consider multiple interpretations before offering an analysis

Such pauses can benefit teachers, as well as students. A short period of silence after one or more students have answered a question enables a teacher to assess the situation, move the conversation forward in non-reactive ways, and ask follow-up questions that involve higher-order thinking.[6] Consistent use of such wait time encourages more deliberate thinking by both teachers and students and enhances the overall quality of discussion in the classroom.

This reflective pausing approach is the hallmark of the teaching style of a middle school educator who is well-versed in slowing down the pace of instruction to "cast a wider net and scoop up more students into becoming engaged in the class." She says that wait time "gives introverts the time needed to process information without the quick verbal processors jumping too quickly into the conversation." It also provides space for ESL learners (English as a Second Language) to feel safe before sharing a thought out loud with the rest of the class. She emphasizes: "It's not an 'accommodation' but a way to 'create space.'"[7]

Table 5.1 summarizes the ways in which several seconds to five minutes of reflective pausing provide the silent context needed to develop a habit for decision-making that is grounded in patience, deliberation, and integrity.

THINK, PAIR, AND SHARE

In 1972, Mary Budd Rowe coined the term "wait time" as a classroom approach to encourage teachers to allow students time to think before responding in order to produce high-quality responses.[8] Her findings about the importance of pausing before accepting answers to questions were extended by Frank Lyman in 1982 with a cooperative learning technique called "Think, Pair, Share."[9] With Think, Pair, Share, students are given time to think on their own, discuss thoughts with a partner, and then share their ideas with the rest of the class as "dynamic duos." This approach allows teachers to ask more in-depth questions that challenge students and provide time for them to think critically in a safe environment. It also encourages students to use higher-order thinking skills to obtain a deeper understanding with more complex answers.[10] The following steps elucidate this deceptively simple introvert-inclusive pedagogical strategy:

1. The teacher poses a question—ideally an open-ended one that requires a critical level of thinking.
2. Each student thinks on their own about this question, jotting down notes. Thinking time should be at least one minute.
3. Students pair up with the person next to them to discuss their ideas for two to five minutes.
4. The teacher invites each pair to share equitably their ideas with the rest of the class.

GROUP WORK: FROM BRAINSTORMING TO BRAINWRITING

In a typical Western classroom design, we often expect our students to do their best work in project-based groups, deploying brainstorming strategies from the 1950s. Legendary advertising mogul Alex Osborn invented the concept of brainstorming, and his principles were deceptively simple: don't judge; be freewheeling; go for quantity; and build on the ideas of fellow members.[11] Brainstorming was designed to spark creativity and productivity in a judgment-free zone of human interaction with a "just talk it out" approach to problem-solving.

Despite its popularity today, research shows that brainstorming techniques from the 1950s do not deliver desired creative outcomes of enhanced group productivity and creativity. When compared with groups of individuals performing independently, studies show that the brainstorming method actually leads to the production of *fewer* and *less-original* ideas. Not only are typical free-for-all brainstorming groups dominated by fear of judgment and the pressure to conform, but research shows that only three people in a group of six to eight tend to do 70 percent of the talking.[12]

Free-for-all brainstorming often results in something called "groupthink," which happens when individuals in project-based groups do not feel comfortable enough to verbally share their ideas with others. The term "groupthink" was coined in the November 1971 edition of *Psychology Today* and is connected with traditional brainstorming strategies that fail to level the "speaking field" for introverts.[13] The result can be decisions that are sparked by the urge to conform to the loudest members of the group, rather than decisions based on input from every member of the group.

Why does this happen to individuals in groups—regardless of personality style? A scientific study by Gregory Berns at Emory University used fMRI brain scans to show that peer pressure changes an individual's perceptions of a problem, even if the individual knew prior to joining the group that the peers' ideas were morally or ethically wrong.[14] Introverts and extroverts alike rally around the first spoken statements in a team meeting or classroom discussion, and peer pressure exerts a pull on the brain that shuts down the impetus for the individual to share ideas that might go against what has just been said. In other words, the power of conformity is such that individuals become chained to the group, eviscerating the diversity of thought that propels teams to be their most productive and creative. Premature consensus is no consensus at all.

Our introverted students are particularly at risk for holding back their opinions in a group. Internal processors who need time to think are not likely to be the first to share ideas on a team that is functioning according to the norms of brainstorming. What we need is a paradigm shift in how we think about group processes—from brainstorming to brainwriting, a relatively new strategy that involves separating idea generation from idea evaluation.[15]

In a brainwriting group, participants start with a period of silent reflection, where team members generate solutions to a problem alone, using as many Post-it notes as possible. After approximately three to five minutes, team members are invited to share their notes on a nearby wall, anonymously, if possible. (See figure 5.3.)

Once similar ideas are grouped together, the evaluation of ideas begins. Which ideas make the most sense and why? Be sure that everyone gets the chance to speak. Build reflective pausing into this entire group conversation by using a "Round Robin" participation technique or by offering those who are more adept at speaking just *three* participation "tokens." Once these three tokens are used up, these vocal participants must make room for others to speak.

During one brainwriting experience with high-school journalists at Columbia University, the author asked students to take a moment to quietly write down their own musings about the "keys to happiness." The silence caused by the lack of speaking was a bit jarring for the participants, as sirens from Broadway filled the room with noise that previously had gone unnoticed. After a few minutes, which seemed like an eternity, students were asked to share their ideas in "dynamic trios." Afterward, the author invited feedback about that moment of quiet reflection. "It was strange, but in a good way," they agreed. The small groups moved on to have fascinating and light-hearted discussions about the secret to happiness.

When asking our students to accomplish tasks in groups, it is also important to choreograph teams so that a balance of introverts and extroverts

Figure 5.3.   Brainwriting is proven to be a more productive and creative option for collaboration than brainstorming. A period of silent "idea generation" allows introverts and extroverts alike to quietly ponder solutions to a problem without the fear of judgment or the pressure to conform. The ensuing "idea evaluation" phase can then be based on contributions from every member of the team. *Kati Haajanen and Esther Aitken.*

translates to real results. According to Rick Howard and Maeve McKillen in "Extraversion and Performance in the Perceptual Maze Test," researchers found that when working on tasks alone, extroversion is associated with faster, less accurate and less reflective performance, while introversion is associated with slower but far more accurate performance.[16] Understanding the social and communication styles of different personality types is the key to leveraging the productivity and creativity of diverse groups of students or educators. Without such understanding, we will lack the basis for building both a healthy sense of respect for others and a strategy for working together harmoniously. The goal is to build a culture of kindness that enables each and every individual to flourish. Ultimately, it falls on each member of the group to ensure that everyone has the chance to be heard.

QUIET-FRIENDLY COMMENTS THAT VALUE SILENCE AS PRELUDE TO TALK

Word choices in anecdotal comments (or progress reports) should indicate to parents that we are experts in understanding temperament diversity. When writing comments about introverted students, we should avoid certain phrases, such as, "He needs to come out of his shell," or, "She doesn't speak up enough in class"; such language can have negative connotations. Instead, we can remark on an introverted student's ability to use techniques from their Long Runway, reflective pausing, or brainwriting "toolboxes" by noting quiet, proactive behaviors that enhance and deepen their learning (and that of others), rather than deficits that suggest that a quiet child needs to be "fixed."

When writing comments about planning and preparation, first consider how a child uses the Long Runway approach to prepare for class. Does she engage in dress rehearsal type activities before presenting ideas to the group? Does he meet with the teacher before and/or after class to ask questions or offer insightful ideas (in person or virtually)? Does she preview topics to strengthen confidence? With constructive feedback, we empower our introverted students to advocate for the preparation time they need to succeed—both at school and in future work settings.

Quiet-Friendly Comment Examples: The Long Runway

- When Mary has a chance to practice presenting information in front of a group, her confidence grows, as does her understanding.
- David often stops by before class to share his thoughts about a homework assignment, and our one-on-one conversations show his depth of understanding of the material.
- Nathan takes time to review study topics for the upcoming week, which allows him to feel both competent and confident during class discussions.
- Mark makes good use of his planning time to develop ideas that are both creative and informative.
- Amy often chooses to follow up on class discussions with insightful comments that she shares via the student/teacher portal, and her comments help to set the stage for the next lesson.

Next, let's consider how students might incorporate reflective pausing into their classroom work. Does she take time to think on her own before asking for help? Does he weigh different options before speaking? Does she carefully consider multiple ideas and think step-by-step through an idea? Does he access prior knowledge before making decisions? By highlighting the benefits of quiet reflection, we empower prudent thinkers to own their strengths.

Quiet-Friendly Comment Examples: Reflective Pausing

- Joshua uses his time wisely to ponder and consider many options before contributing to class discussions.
- Bonnie's written responses demonstrate an understanding of the content and an ability to analyze information.
- When Tina pauses to organize her thoughts before speaking, she demonstrates a depth of understanding.
- When Isaac speaks in class discussions, his comments reflect careful analysis and understanding.
- Matthew knows how to use his planning time wisely and will often jot down his thoughts and ideas in order to be prepared for class discussions.

Finally, when writing anecdotal comments, we can note and appreciate the ways in which our introverted students naturally engage in group work, drawing on their strengths of listening and observing to contribute positively to group functionality. Does he form meaningful relationships? Does she extend group understanding with insightful questions? Does she listen carefully to others' ideas? Does his body language express interest and understanding? Over time, the practice of brainwriting can promote a sense of belonging for all members of a team.

Quiet-Friendly Comment Examples: Group Work

- When "brainwriting," Coco takes full advantage of silent reflection time to come up with numerous innovative ideas to share later with the group.
- During group work, Faris listens carefully to his classmates. He is skilled in knowing how to provide opportunities for each participant to speak and share ideas.
- Nicolas' empathic awareness of his classmates' needs and their interactions within the group enables him to moderate group projects in a thoughtful, diplomatic manner.

- Daisy's empathic listening skills enable her to ask questions that extend her classmates' understanding, especially during small-group projects.
- Berta demonstrates engagement during group work by taking thorough notes, making eye contact, and nodding when someone is speaking.

We will explore more ways to build connections with parents (in addition to written comments) and show our commitment to introvert-friendly classrooms in the next chapter on parent–school partnerships.

REFLECTIONS: MICRO-MINDFUL MOMENTS

"I was quiet, but I was not blind."—Jane Austen

LONG RUNWAY

1. Have you—or other members of your family—ever had an experience with needing additional time to prepare to "take flight?" Were you—or they—able to carve out the time needed? Why or why not?
2. How does your own personality style affect your thinking about the Long Runway? How challenging is it for you to provide this sort of lead time for your students? How challenging is it for you to provide this sort of lead time for your students?:
3. Which one of the following scenarios do you prefer? Why?
A. On Sunday, your partner gives you a list of potential activities for the weekend ahead.
B. On Friday, your partner wants to try something "new and exciting" on Saturday.

REFLECTIVE PAUSING

1. Do you currently practice "wait time" as part of your pedagogy? If not, how might you incorporate reflective pausing into your teaching practice?
2. Will it be a challenge to shift culture around the idea of "quiet times" in your school or organization? Or is this practice already embedded in your culture? Explain.

GROUP WORK

"I help my students understand that theater is an ensemble. It's a group of individuals working toward a common goal. And in that ensemble, one person is no more important than another. And I treat every member of the ensemble that way, and I think that that really helps the introverted kids not to feel like they are in the background." Upper School Theater Director[17]

1. Do you ever see yourself managing your classroom like an ensemble?
2. How often do you provide opportunities for rotating team leadership on teams—assigning roles to individual members or having them assign roles themselves? Explain.
3. What do you see as the benefits of the brainwriting approach to creative collaboration?

QUIET-FRIENDLY COMMENTS

Read the examples provided, noting the extrovert bias in each one. Next, rewrite the examples. Note that this reflection can serve as the basis for a faculty meeting prior to comment/report writing time.

- Example to revise—Carole is quiet but completes her work efficiently.
- Example of rewrite—Carole is an efficient and thorough student, completing her work on time, if not sooner.

Comments to revise:

1. Raymond needs to come out of his shell and contribute during class discussions.
2. Bob respects his classmates, but he only participates in class discussions periodically.
3. While Elizabeth is respectful of her classmates, she is hesitant to share her thoughts during class discussions.
4. Karen has many ideas but never shares them during class discussions.

Chapter 6

Parent–School Partnerships

"Think and wonder, wonder and think."—Dr. Seuss

It's common today for parents to feel that their introverted child is misunderstood in school. Class participation grades that assess the quantity over the quality of speech are a key reason for such parental complaints, as well as anecdotal comments that seemingly shame children for not speaking up. As we foster quiet-friendly school cultures, using techniques in class such as the Long Runway, reflective pausing, and brainwriting (see chapter 5), it is important to build healthy parent–school partnerships as part of the process.

Effective teaching requires knowledge of the whole child—academically, socially, and emotionally. In "The Parent-School Partnership: Optimizing Relationships and Building Understanding," Olaf Jorgenson advocates for strengthening the parent–teacher connection in a deliberate fashion to avoid what is often the "default mode" for this relationship: "Us versus Them." In the article, Jorgenson states that in coauthoring *Raising Kids: Your Essential Guide to Everyday Parenting* with family therapist and school consultant Sheri Glucoft Wong, he started with the premise that it is of paramount importance to cultivate positive connections with parents to strengthen shared purpose and community schoolwide. It's the parents who are experts in who their children are as individuals and the teachers who are experts in specific childhood developmental stages.[1] Together, parents and schools can work to optimize the growth of the child.

The ideal parent–school partnership is one that enables parents to feel seen and heard, on the one hand, and allows teachers to offer honest feedback about the child's behaviors, on the other. The more information that is openly shared between schools and parents, either virtually or in person, the more support can be given to the student. With parent and teacher knowledge combined, both parties can better nurture the whole child.

TALKING POINTS FOR CONVERSATIONS WITH PARENTS ABOUT INTROVERTED CHILDREN

Communication "toolkits" can help educators effectively interact with parents of introverted children during conferences or meetings and, in so doing, help to build quiet-friendly school cultures. It's critical to have the language needed to talk to families about introverts; parents of introverted children often ask educators what they can do at home to nurture their child. Educators can prepare for these meetings with a few talking points about parenting introverted children: setting structure through routines; creating quiet spaces at home; providing a Long Runway for social events; and establishing a family book club. (See figure 6.1.)

Figure 6.1. It's important for educators to prepare talking points in advance of parent-teacher conferences in order to ensure that caregivers can nurture their introverted child at home in a manner that is consistent with best educational practices for introverted students. *Kati Haajanen and Esther Aitken.*

Before offering parenting advice during a conference or meeting, however, it is advisable to ask a few questions first about their child's behaviors at home. This will help in answering appropriately the frequently asked question, "What can I do at home to best support my introverted child?" and set the stage for parent–school teamwork. Possible questions include:

- Why do you consider your child to be an introvert?
- Does your child tend to feel anxious or enthusiastic about the start of the school year?
- What is your child's favorite part of school?
- What is your child's least favorite part of school?
- Does your child have any routines at home? After school? At bedtime? In the morning? At homework time?

SETTING STRUCTURE THROUGH ROUTINES

Psychotherapist Marti Olsen Laney provides many suggestions for parents of introverted children in her book *The Hidden Gifts of the Introverted Child—Helping Your Child Thrive in an Extroverted World*. Laney encourages parents to observe and understand their introverted child by noting patterns in their daily energy levels and by providing routines. Creating home routines, such as regular morning and after-school schedules, produces a safe environment for the introverted child. Laney encourages parents to be aware of the "most active" and "slowest" times of day for their child, as well as the conditions in which the child thrives. Keeping a schedule, without surprises and with time for recharging, allows the introverted child to live in an environment geared to their needs.[2]

In her book *Quiet Kids—Help Your Introverted Child Succeed in an Extroverted World*, educational psychologist Christine Fonseca makes recommendations on how to create an ideal home environment for an introvert. She suggests a calm, organized, and clutter-free environment in which routines and predictable schedules are provided, along with time for solitude. Parents can model positive routines in their own lives and support their introverted child with regular times for healthy meals and snacks, work time, and downtime. Additional ideas include reducing social pressure when the child is overextended and serving meals with balanced choices (that include protein) at regular intervals.[3]

CREATING QUIET SPACES AT HOME

Since introverts need alone time to recharge, parents can be encouraged to think about how to set up the home to meet their introverted child's need for a quiet space. Including the child in decisions related to these arrangements provides the child with both a sense of ownership and a feeling of safety. Parents can invite their child to co-create a cozy space inside the home for recharging: a comfortable chair in the corner of a room, a hidden reading space, or a tent-like structure are usually popular options for introverts. If an outdoor space is available, parents and children can discuss various options for designating or creating a peaceful spot where the child can be alone without worrying about "loner" labels: a treehouse, a "secret garden," a swing, or a bench. It is also important to provide a quiet and calm space for homework, where the child has control over light and noise in the designated work area. (See figure 6.2.)

As these conversations unfold, we should be mindful of the fact that it can be challenging for an extroverted parent or caregiver to separate their own needs from those of their introverted child, particularly when it comes to divergent recharging styles. Witness the story of an extroverted mother of twins (one introverted and one extroverted) who became worried when her introverted daughter wanted to have her own room: "I started to get concerned about her. She wanted to move up to the third floor in our house in first grade. She stayed up there a lot and would want to be by herself a lot."

This mother of twins continues, "I made the mistake, which I now know not to do, of thinking that something was wrong. My other daughter was friendly and seemed to be very comfortable with people. My introverted one wasn't unfriendly, but she wasn't as outgoing, and she was totally comfortable being up in her room reading." She candidly adds, "I pushed her into situations that I now know were not the right thing to do. It came completely out of what I thought was best for her and my love for her." She concludes,

Figure 6.2. Introverts need time alone to recharge, and parents can invite their child to co-create a quiet space inside or outside the home. *Kati Haajanen and Esther Aitken.*

"I fully understand now that my daughter needs recharge time. And if she doesn't get it, it's really uncomfortable for her."[4]

PROVIDING A LONG RUNWAY FOR SOCIAL EVENTS

In addition to guidance about quiet spaces, educators can offer suggestions to parents as they prepare their introverted child for family or school-related social events. There are many techniques to make the transition easier when attending a social gathering, and each can be offered as a way to provide a Long Runway (see chapter 5).

- Practice and rehearse prior to attending the event; talk about what will happen and how to be involved.
- Arrive early if it is possible and socially acceptable.
- Discuss the possible positive opportunities and outcomes that will come from this event.
- Find out prior to the event whether close friends or relatives will be attending.
- Encourage and practice taking breaks during social events.
- Debrief after a social event by discussing what felt good and what they might want to work on or practice for future gatherings.
- Create opportunities to practice low-risk, comfortable "stretch" behaviors, such as small talk with a store clerk (see chapter 3).

Encouraging parents to embrace these techniques will help to build the introverted child's confidence and comfort level, especially when a large, unfamiliar social gathering is on the family calendar. One elementary school director interviewed for the book often shares with families about a time when her introverted daughter was invited to a neighbor's pool during summer vacation, and she preferred to sit quietly and read rather than splash with others in the water. Instead of asking her daughter, "What is wrong with you? Why aren't you swimming with your friends?" she validated her daughter's need to have the space and time and do what was comfortable for her. She summarizes, "Parents who don't have awareness of personality diversity tend to push their kids in ways that aren't helpful to the child's confidence and demeanor."[5]

ESTABLISHING A FAMILY BOOK CLUB

Literature provides an opportunity to learn about introversion/extroversion through the journeys of different characters and how they cope with diverse situations and relationships. With appropriate book suggestions, parents can connect with their introverted child when the family chooses to read a book together. An ensuing discussion can enable children to see how both introverts and extroverts deal with a variety of life situations.

Family reading time provides opportunities to share thoughts by "visiting" new worlds, creating a comfortable parent/child routine in the process. Educators can counsel parents to ask their child the following crucial question: "Which character do you relate to the most and why?" Parents can extend the discussion by then asking their child about their feelings or reactions to other characters and events or the story's setting. The following list of questions is designed to help families get started with the discussion:

- What personality qualities help you connect with a certain character? How does this character interact with other characters in the story?
- Which character do you dislike or disagree with the most? Why?
- Describe a situation in the story that you remember vividly.
  ○ What were your feelings while you were reading about this situation?
  ○ How was it resolved?
  ○ If you were the author, would you have resolved it in the same way?

Reading together should be an informal, comfortable time to share a love of literature and the stories and adventures that come with it. A plethora of books is available, both picture and chapter books, that are rich in introverted character development. For young children, picture books and wordless books create opportunities for pausing during the story to talk about characters and their relationships. As children begin reading chapter books, concepts and relationships become more interwoven, providing the potential for rich discussions about people's identities and life's opportunities and challenges. With older children, chapter books can be read together as a family, or a parent and child can each read the book on their own and share thoughts after a few chapters. Note that this same technique of learning about temperament types through literature can be applied to movies and cartoons.

PRESCHOOL AND ELEMENTARY SCHOOL LITERATURE

Winnie-the-Pooh, a well-known book that has been enjoyed by readers of many ages throughout the years, is perfect for learning about different temperament types through literature. Winnie continually works on "figuring out" life among his friends. As a character who displays introverted personality preferences, he enjoys his "comfy" time at home, and he also knows that it is important to venture out to the forest to be with his friends; he comes to realize that he should not always expect Owl (more introverted), Piglet (more extroverted), or Tigger (more extroverted) to stop by for a visit. As the characters of the forest discuss friendships and life, their dialogue provides the perfect reading material to better understand interactions between introverts and extroverts.[6]

The following list provides some additional suggestions of books for this age group:

- *The Ugly Duckling* by Hans Christian Andersen
- *Miss Rumphius* by Barbara Cooney
- *The Mouse Scouts* series by Sarah Dillard
- *Shh! We Have a Plan* by Chris Haughton
- *The Story of Ferdinand* by Munro Leaf
- *Frog and Toad* series by Arnold Lobel
- *The Magic Tree House* series by Mary Pope Osborne
- *The Cat in the Hat* by and other books by Dr. Seuss
- *Max and Ruby* books by Rosemary Wells
- *The Velveteen Rabbit* by Margery Williams
- *Love Birds* by Jane Yolen

MIDDLE SCHOOL LITERATURE

Many other books, including chapter books, provide valuable and rich examples of how introverts deal with friendships and challenging situations. In Roald Dahl's *Matilda*, the main character, Matilda, who displays introverted personality preferences, discovers ways to best interact with her more extroverted parents, brother, and headmistress. As a voracious reader, Matilda finds comfort in her books and becomes a favorite with the librarians. She develops a special bond with her teacher, Miss Jennifer Honey, a fellow introvert with a mild and quiet temperament. When visiting Miss Honey at her cottage, Matilda becomes "wildly animated" and eager to talk one-on-one.[7] In the classroom, Matilda protects her classmates from bullies, and her maturity and ability to analyze situations enable her to work through difficult situations with others. While many of Matilda's adventures are exaggerated in the book, it is filled with adventures and opportunities for discussing how an introverted character faces and overcomes challenges.

The following list provides some additional suggestions for this age group:

- *The Secret Garden* by Frances Hodgson Burnett
- *Chasing Redbird* by Sharon Creech

- *The BFG* and other books by Roald Dahl
- *King of the Wind* by Marguerite Henry
- *The Moomins* series of books by Tove Jansson
- *The Phantom Tollbooth* by Norton Juster
- *From the Mixed-up Files of Mrs. Basil E. Frankweiler* by E.L. Konigsburg
- *A Wrinkle in Time* by Madeleine L'Engle
- *Bridge to Terabithia* by Katherine Paterson
- *Harry Potter* series by J. K. Rowling
- *Call It Courage* by Armstrong Sperry

HIGH-SCHOOL LITERATURE

For older students, Bilbo Baggins is often considered to be a true introvert who is hesitant to try something very unfamiliar—such as going on an adventure with the wizard Gandalf in *The Hobbit*. Bilbo enjoys his Hobbit home and feels comfortable with his friends and the neighborhood. At first, he is reluctant to go on Gandalf's trip, shunning a journey that will come with many surprises, but once Bilbo gets started, he discovers that he can do it—and that he works well with others. As his confidence grows, through successfully surmounting challenges, Bilbo gains many new friends. In the end, Bilbo returns home to his cozy space. Both parents and teenagers will find many discussion points about an introvert's interactions with others and ways to confront new situations as they read and discuss the adventures of Bilbo and his friends.[8]

The following list provides some additional suggestions for this age group:

- *Little Women* by Louisa May Alcott
- *Pride and Prejudice* by Jane Austen
- *Jane Eyre* by Charlotte Bronte
- *The Hunger Games* by Suzanne Collins
- *All the Light We Cannot See* by Anthony Doerr
- *The Diary of a Young Girl* by Anne Frank
- *Cate of the Lost Colony* by Lisa Klein
- *Where the Crawdads Sing* by Delia Owens
- *The Goldfinch* by Donna Tartt
- *Walden* by Henry David Thoreau
- *Anna Karenina* by Leo Tolstoy
- *Waves* and other books by Virginia Woolf
- *The Book Thief* by Markus Zusak

Parent–School Partnerships 77

Figure 6.3. School-sponsored book clubs unite parents with a common interest in raising introverted children. *Kati Haajanen and Esther Aitken.*

PARENTS TOGETHER: A SCHOOL-SPONSORED BOOK CLUB

To extend understanding of temperament diversity beyond parent–teacher conferences and occasional emails or phone calls, educators can experiment with the old-fashioned method of setting up a "lending library" with books or articles on introvert-inclusivity and nurturing quiet leaders that parents can access easily when they are in the schoolhouse. To encourage communication within the parent body about these resources, educators can use this library as a springboard for sponsoring a book club that unites those with a common interest in raising introverted kids. Ideally, a parent or caregiver—rather than a teacher, administrator, or counselor—is in charge of moderating a quarterly book club discussion. In this way, parents have ownership in building community around nurturing introverted children. (See figure 6.3.)

PARENTS TOGETHER: SCHOOL-SPONSORED QUIET COFFEES

Establishing parent gatherings at school is another effective way to encourage parents and caregivers to delve more deeply into understanding introverted learners, while at the same time creating an environment where families can share stories and learn from one another. At one all-girls school, parent coffees are held three times throughout the school year. The first meeting of the year always includes an overview of the qualities and needs of an introvert.

Using a question-and-answer format, families learn from one another and share techniques that they find useful for their children. The gatherings create a forum for open communication and provide language and techniques for effectively supporting introverted children.[9]

When planning such a gathering, it is useful to consider the logistics first. Is it best to have a meeting first thing in the morning after dropping students off at school? Would lunchtime or after school be better? Will an in-person gathering reach more participants, or is a virtual meeting a better approach? Posting an invitation through various venues will reach more family members and will also serve as a reminder for them. Pre-registration is advised since it helps to create a sense of commitment.

After the first meeting, expand on the topic of temperament diversity by focusing on specific themes, highlighting the ways in which the school is tending to the needs of introverted students by using quiet-friendly pedagogical approaches. Be sure to start any subsequent presentation with a review of an introvert's qualities and needs. In this way, returning families have the chance to revisit important concepts, and new participants are provided with necessary background information on personality types.

Another essential topic to explore with parents involves the ways in which your school or organization values quiet spaces. "Rescuing Solitude" is the theme of the next two chapters.

REFLECTIONS: MICRO-MINDFUL MOMENTS

"I think a lot, but I don't say much."—Anne Frank

FORGING PARENT–SCHOOL PARTNERSHIPS

1. What is your preferred way to communicate with parents?
2. Describe a successful meeting or conference that you have had with parents of an introverted child. What made it successful?
3. Describe a meeting or a conference with a parent that did not go well. What happened? What can you learn from this example?
4. Are there any changes that you recommend for strengthening relationships with parents while still respecting communication boundaries (such as "no emails after a certain time of the day" or "texting is prohibited")?

TALKING POINTS FOR CONVERSATIONS WITH PARENTS OF INTROVERTED CHILDREN

1. Which talking points in this chapter resonated the most with you? Why? Do you have others?
2. Think of positive interactions you have had recently with an introverted student. How can this story become an example that you use with other parents to demonstrate your understanding of an introverted student's personality style and the ways in which you and your school address those needs?

TALKING POINTS: SPOTLIGHT ON PROVIDING A LONG RUNWAY FOR SOCIAL EVENTS

"My parents were always good about encouraging me to attend social activities but not go beyond my limit, even if I didn't want to do it. They'd say, 'Just go for twenty minutes and come home. You will be fine.' It always felt kind, very supportive, and that made it easier."—Elementary School Teacher[10]

1. How might you use this example in a parent–teacher conference or meeting?
2. When might this approach be a practical one, and when might this parental advice not be possible (for instance, when it's important to stay longer than twenty minutes at a certain social gathering)? In the latter case, what might you advise parents to say to an introverted child?
3. Have you ever felt this way yourself? Have you ever taken an "Irish exit" at a social event (leaving early without notifying others)?

ESTABLISHING A FAMILY BOOK CLUB

1. Among the books on the lists provided in this chapter, which ones resonate with you the most as ways to connect with introverted children? Why would you suggest that parents read this one alongside their introverted child?
2. How might you encourage parents to use literature as a way to help their child learn more about temperament diversity?
3. Which books—or movies—might you add to these lists?

PARENT COFFEES

1. Does your school have a framework in place to offer virtual or in-person parent educational programs on temperament diversity? If so, what works well when the programs are offered? What might work better?
2. If needed, how can you help organize a parent education program that focuses on spreading knowledge about temperament types, with an emphasis on introverted students and their needs? How can you—and others—make the time for this sort of endeavor?

Section III

RESCUING SOLITUDE

Chapter 7

Benefits of Solitude

"We live, in fact, in a world starved for solitude, silence, and privacy: and therefore starved for mediation and true friendship."—C.S. Lewis

AVOIDING SOLITUDE

Modern life has taught us to avoid solitude. As a result, words such as "reclusive" and "lonely" may be used to describe someone who seeks alone time, even in public spaces. A 2014 research study published in the journal *Science* found that participants typically did not enjoy spending six to fifteen minutes in a room by themselves with nothing to do but think. In order to avoid being alone with their thoughts, about two-thirds of the men and one-quarter of the women in the study chose to administer mild electric shocks to themselves, rather than do "nothing."[1]

Why might this be true? The answer comes as no surprise. According to Leigh Marz and Justin Zorn in "How to Build a Culture that Honors Quiet Time," there is empirical evidence to show that life today is noisier than ever before, from televisions to loudspeakers, and from electronic device notifications to open-floor-plan offices.[2] In *Golden: The Power of Silence of a World of Noise*, Marz and Zorn define "noise" as any unwelcome interference in our lives—at the informational, auditory, and internal levels of our perception.[3] There are inimical effects of such unwelcome—and often excessive—stimulation on the human psyche—for introverts and extroverts alike. Marz and Zorn claim it is more difficult than ever to make intentional, meaningful decisions and to integrate ourselves with the outside world. Without quiet times, we are living fragmented, distracted, and interrupted lives.[4]

With opportunities for constant informational connection, we are tempted at every moment of the day to view YouTube videos, respond to text messages, and post photos and videos on Instagram. Studies show that our dependence on digital activity that *instantaneously* connects us with others is at an all-time high. Regardless of age, the percentage of Americans saying that they would feel anxious if they lost their phone for the day, a potential marker of smartphone addiction, has held steady over the years at 44 percent in 2022, compared to 42 percent in 2015.[5]

When it comes to being distracted by information, a bright billboard on the side of the highway is another case in point. Driving along the freeway, trying to focus on maintaining a constant speed and avoiding the occasional wayward vehicle, one can easily be distracted by neon lights that shine in the name of some product that one should consider purchasing at a low, low price! (See figure 7.1.) When the police sirens are blaring behind you, you realize that you unintentionally exceeded the speed limit while looking at that neon sign.

As for auditory noise, let's focus on both throughways and airports. As Melissa Dahl reports in "How Prolonged Exposure to Sweet, Blessed Silence Benefits the Brain (2016)," the term "noise pollution" was coined in the 1960s when scientists found that the loud sounds from roads and planes are associated with a myriad of health concerns, including high blood pressure, sleep loss, and heart disease.[6]

Further studies corroborate this thesis that auditory noise can threaten human well-being. As reported by Mariann Szegedy-Maszak in a 2005 *Los Angeles Times* article, researchers from Johns Hopkins University found that

Figure 7.1. A bright billboard can be distracting for drivers who are trying to focus on the road ahead or preparing to take a turn needed to get to their destination. Visual noise can not only lead to speeding tickets, but to accidents en route. *Kati Haajanen and Esther Aitken.*

"excessive" noise in hospitals (or noise that exceeds thirty-five decibels, as established by the World Health Organization) from such things as beeping instruments and ventilation systems inhibit a patient's ability to recover.[7] Such noise can cause harm, including high blood pressure and increased risk of heart attack, in a place dedicated specifically to healing.

What about auditory noise in schools? A 2023 study by Gary Rance, Richard C. Dowell, and Dani Tomlin affirms that the open-plan classroom, an "anti-authoritarian" design from the 1960s and 1970s, has a myriad of unintended "authoritarian" effects on learning. As they report, intrusive noise from classrooms in surrounding areas reduces speech intelligibility. Speech perception, according to their study, is impaired by the background noise that comes with an open plan, where "classrooms" are separated by flimsy dividers. It is harder to listen and thus harder to both receive and process information. This study is particularly relevant to the development of literacy in seven- to ten-year-old students: Reading fluency development is greater for students being taught in enclosed classrooms than it is for those in open-classroom environments.[8]

Inner monologues, which often include negative self-talk, can dominate our soundscape as much as external noise, causing anxiety and other forms of psychological distress. Based on Ethan Kross' research on the science of internal dialogue in *Chatter: The Voice in Our Head, Why It Matters, and How to Harness It*, internal interference from our own minds can turn what might otherwise be a peaceful moment of respite into an experience akin to being bullied on a playground.[9]

THE PLENITUDE OF SOLITUDE

Imagine a world free from the external and internal forces that distract us from self-examination. Such a world enables us to be awake to our thoughts and our surroundings, fueling our ability to lead life with purpose—and interact more intentionally with others.

Witness the literary testimonial of Henry David Thoreau when he ventured into the woods in Concord, Massachusetts, to live deliberately alone, fueling his ability to write his masterpiece, *Walden*, with wakeful attention to both his inner thoughts and nature. As Margot Wielgus, Thomas Bohn, and Gunter Figal affirm in "Solitude and Thinking: Henry David Thoreau" (2017), Thoreau posited that it is only when we are disengaged from societal norms and values that we are able to engage with the self in profound ways. In such a state of solitude, we are better able to think for ourselves and come up with the original ideas that are the foundation of innovative work.[10]

It is important to note that it is possible to be solitary in society. As Diana Senechal affirms in *The Republic of Noise: The Loss of Solitude in Schools and Culture*, Thoreau believed that one can find solitude anywhere, even in a crowded lecture hall. It's the "solitude of the mind" that truly matters, or the willingness to turn inward and to think for oneself, and have a mind apart from others.[11] Solitude is a catalyst for mindful awareness, innovation, compassion, and authentic joy.

SOLITUDE AS THE SETTING FOR SILENCE

The solitude that we are exploring in this book is one that is connected to silence, where there is no intake of information from the outside world. Playing headphones with music, podcasts, or news prohibits us from the benefits of solitary silence.

In a 2014 *Nautilus* article, science writer Daniel A. Gross notes that prolonged exposure to silence has health benefits. He highlights a 2013 study by Duke University's Imke Kirste, which demonstrated that two hours of silence a day prompts cell development in the hippocampus, the brain region associated with the formation of memory (involving the senses).[12] Given that depression is related in part to the slowing of cell growth in the hippocampus, it is not surprising that psychologist Reed Larson found that adolescents who spend more time alone are less likely to be depressed.[13] During this prolonged and repeated exposure to silence, when the brain rests quietly, we allow ourselves the time to be less reactive to complex situations in our social and digital worlds, instead gathering ourselves and our thoughts to later share with others. Paradoxically, solitude leads us to form deeper connections with others, provided that we are ready to join the conversation.

Gross goes on to explain what happens to the brain when it is exposed to noise at unacceptable sound levels (such as the seventy-two decibels often found in hospitals). He describes that neurophysiological research indicates that noise first activates the amygdala, clusters of neurons located in the temporal lobes of the brain that are affiliated with emotion, and that this activation prompts an immediate release of stress hormones like cortisol, even during sleep.[14] A good night's sleep is a prized commodity: witness the robust market in America for noise-canceling headphones and sound machines. If we can't have quiet in our midst, we need to manufacture it!

Finally, Gross cites the astounding 2006 research of physician Luciano Bernardi about the physiological effects of silent interludes when listening to musical scores. While Bernardi found that listening to music activates conditions of arousal, as it requires alertness and attention, he also discovered that a two-minute break in between musical recordings offers the listener more relaxation than was provided by actually listening to "relaxing music"—as long as the break comes as a brief intermission between songs.[15] As it turns out, playing "relaxing" music non-stop does not allow the brain the time it needs to settle down. It's the silence, the sharp break from sound, that allows the auditory cortex to settle into a state of relative inactivity.

SOLITUDE AND RECHARGING

In addition to improving our health, exposing ourselves to periods of solitude can help us regain our balance, or well-being, whenever necessary. Dr. Brian Little coined the term "restorative niche" to describe a physical or mental place where we go to recuperate after flexing outside our comfort zone; it's the place we go to return to our true selves.[16] For an extroverted educator who has just spent a free period preparing for afternoon classes, recharging could include spending time in a busy lunchroom. For an introverted educator who has just taught three periods in a row, recharging might mean spending solitary time meditating.

In a 2005 article, "Personal Projects and Free Traits," Little writes that "for a biogenic introvert who has been protractedly acting out of character as a 'pseudo-extravert,' the best restorative niche would be one of solitude and reduced stimulation."[17] Taking time alone to restore is not synonymous with antisocial behavior; it is essential for the well-being of introverts in school environments, which are notoriously busy and noisy places that often demand a schedule that does not allow for quiet rejuvenation. As one educator affirms, "I had a student who would come down to my classroom periodically and just say, 'I just need to recharge here,' because it was quiet. And I tried to make spaces in the room for the kids to recharge."[18]

Understanding one's need for recharging time can begin as early as the toddler years. (See figure 7.2.) A social studies educator from the Northeast reminisces about her childhood restorative niche:

> I think my mom will tell the story that when I was a toddler, I would ask for "privy time," privacy time just to be by myself. And so it's been a part of me. I never really could name or figure out why I needed it, what the benefit was, but I knew it helped me. And as I learned more over the years about being an introvert, it really just made sense to me that that's really what was happening all along.[19]

Likewise, another self-aware educator, who defines herself as a "classic introvert," recognizes that she needs recharge time during the school day. After getting "a lot of energy from collaborating with colleagues," she has to set aside quiet alone time. She states,

Figure 7.2. Allow introverts the space they need for privacy at home. It is essential for recharging and enables them to engage more fully in social events. *Kati Haajanen and Esther Aitken.*

> I need time just to be, which is often sitting in formal meditation practice or just sitting in the garden and being with nature. Without the recharge time, I find I can get irritable, cranky, and have less patience. I need to make sure that I carve out a few minutes of absolute quiet time for myself in order to be able to re-engage in a meaningful way.[20]

The more we understand that a fundamental part of being human is finding our "sweet spot" between calm and excitement, the healthier and more able we will be to go out into the world and make a difference.

BUILDING IN RECHARGE TIME AT THE START OF CLASS

Accessing a "restorative niche" may not be easy, given school schedules, which, more often than not, are supercharged with classes and activities. As a result, students often do not have the chance to quietly recharge on their own. This is especially true of middle- and high-school students, who tend not to have a designated "homeroom" space and thus are constantly moving from one classroom to the next. This can be nothing short of exhausting, particularly for introverted students, many of whom have heard about the "good old days" when desks with a large compartment for their personal belongings were placed in rows, and students stayed in one room for the entire day.

While we may not be able to go back in time, we can help our students today by intentionally carving out that alone time *for them*. One middle-school teacher provides five minutes of quiet relaxation time at the beginning of each class so that students can "integrate themselves into the environment" in order to be fully present for the start of a lesson. What might be construed as "giving up time" is, in fact, giving students the "gift of time" so that they can let go of whatever happened in the past and sink themselves into the present moment of learning. As she avers,

> Instead of being expected to fully switch to a brand new group of people with a brand new setup, let the students have quiet time. They will feel as though it helps them to be fully present where they are, ready to engage in a novel learning environment.[21]

This accommodation for switching environments also helps extroverted students. Regardless of temperament, all students need time for their nervous systems to acclimate to a new learning situation.

BUILDING IN RECHARGE TIME AFTER SCHOOL

It's just as important to create time for recharging after school as it is before class starts. One director of an elementary after-school program allows students to take forty-five minutes to simply go outside to play, even if they have homework to complete before pickup time. "I'd say 'Just go out, and when we come back in, we will get it done. It's not a problem, but you need to go and play.'" She continues, "Once they go outside, it's just so wonderful to see them relaxing, running, and jumping or dancing. They're able to let out all that stress. They think better and they get their homework done."[22]

However, well-meaning parents can object to using after-school programs for this sort of unstructured activity, believing this time offers yet another opportunity for their children to grow and develop academically. Sometimes, introverted children simply cannot take on more activities, regardless of whether the activities are academic or extracurricular. When introverted children are asked to do too much, they can become frustrated and withdraw because they simply don't have the energy.

This after-school teacher continues: "If yet another challenge is presented after school, children may just burst out into tears because it's just too much. They feel you're asking them to do one more thing and they don't want to do it."[23] When children don't yet have the skills to self-advocate for recharge time, it's incumbent upon educators to help parents understand that they might be overscheduling their child.

For our older students, advisory can provide opportunities for deep discussions about energy management after school. A high-school theater teacher states, "We literally sat down and scheduled a recharge time, because if my advisee, who was a lead in the play, didn't have it scheduled, she didn't do it." With the knowledge that she would have just twenty minutes to listen to her favorite music or podcast in her bedroom, the advisee reported feeling more relaxed, less anxious, and refreshed for the next performance. She continues, "It's important to actually make yourself *make* the time. Just like my workout. If I don't schedule my workout, well, it's not going to happen!"[24]

This introvert-friendly educator does the same for all of her students before a theatrical performance when they are typically "flying off the walls . . . it's chatter, chatter, chatter, music, music, music." And, as she adds,

> I have students for whom that's not going to work. So I give them a separate space where they can go, where there's no audience . . . they can be where they are. As long as the stage manager knows where they are, they can be in another place.[25]

She also reserves forty minutes for her actors to engage in quiet relaxation time before a curtain call, citing the benefits of this "turning inward time" for both her introverts and extroverts.

SOLITUDE AND RESILIENCE

How do we help our students to be more resilient? We often think of resilience as a character strength that can grow with effort by simply trying harder or practicing longer. While this may be true in some circumstances, there is another part of the story: solitude. As Shawn Achor and Michelle Gielan posit in "Resilience Is about How You Recharge, Not about How You Endure (2016)," a resilient child is a well-rested one. Overwork and exhaustion are the opposite of resilience.[26] A resilient child is more self-aware and thus able to self-regulate their emotions, as well as excel on a test.

Resilience fundamentally has to do with rebalancing. It's the skill of noticing our own thoughts and unhooking from the non-constructive ones so that we can see setbacks as opportunities for growth. The opposite of resilience is perfectionism. In other words, the more you lean toward perfectionism, the harder it will be for you to recover whenever you encounter difficulties in life. According to Dr. JoAnn Deak, "Perfectionism shuts down the resilience part of the brain."[27] We need to convey to our students that they don't have to be "perfect" all of the time and that we can only be at peace with our mistakes when we examine them and learn from them with an open mind—not bury them.

To build resilience in our students, a good place to start is digital breaks. In "How Technology Can Be Part of a Happy Life (2021)," Amy Blankson advises us to start each day with a list of digital intentions to avoid the trap of constant distraction from our electronic devices. How much time do I want to spend online today? When will I turn off notifications and for how long? She notes the alarming fact that it takes eleven minutes to get back into the flow of work after spending just two seconds reading a text message.[28]

Just as it can be seemingly "antisocial" to take a digital break, taking a social break at school is often equated with "loner" behavior. Yet, both are essential to our well-being. Teachers can serve as role models in conveying the importance of solitude. As one elementary school educator affirms,

> It was draining for me to keep the lunch conversation going after teaching all morning. And so I finally got to a point where I said, "Girls, you're welcome to start a conversation or play a game . . . but I just need some quiet time today. I just need to eat." And they've always been very responsive to that and I think it's given permission for others at my table to feel like that's okay too.[29]

SOLITUDE AND CREATIVITY

Whereas solitude boosts resilience, it is imperative to creativity. Creativity is the capacity within individuals to develop ideas for the purpose of solving problems. While creativity is regarded as a valuable and highly coveted skill, its realization remains elusive, particularly in schools where high-stakes testing determines the learning environment. Students in the United States get back hundreds of assignments each year from their teachers. As a result, professional development often focuses on assessment and standards, with the facilitation of creativity seemingly at odds with testing goals.[30]

This happens despite extensive brain research that points to the fact that exercising imagination helps improve long-term retention of information. With imagination and creativity, information is encoded by the brain in ways that make it personally meaningful and thus more memorable. The belief that a disconnect exists between cognitive and creative functions—the brain's executive control network and the imagination network—creates a false dichotomy. Both are needed to maximize human potential and the ability to innovate.[31]

How can educators create opportunities for students to unleash their imaginations? As humanistic psychologist Scott Barry Kaufman asserts in *Wired to Create*, the answer is solitude, as solitude enables the inward elements of our brain to function optimally.[32] As Susan Cain mentions in a 2015 *Scientific American* article, some of the most creative people in any field are introverts since they tend to be comfortable spending time alone, and solitude is a crucial ingredient for creativity.[33]

While it may be more natural for introverts than for extroverts to seek out alone time, it is critical to create solitary experiences for students of all personality styles in order to foster creativity. Given the pervasiveness of the extrovert ideal—collaboration and noise—in our school cultures, we need to normalize solitude by intentionally teaching students about its benefits, which include the following:

- The ability to think about one thing at a time. Multitasking has been shown to dilute the quality and efficiency of what we're trying to accomplish.[34]
- The ability to recognize creative impulses and pursue them, free from distracting stimuli.
- The ability to take in new forms of information, art, and beauty without being encumbered by others' opinions of it.

Solitude creates the ideal context for the state of flow, a psychological state characterized by complete absorption, concentration, joy, and a subjective loss of time. As psychologist Mihaly Csikszentmihalyi's research demonstrates, flow is an optimal state in which one feels totally engaged in an activity. In this state, the individual is free from rewards—money, status, and prestige. When in flow, all aspects of performance are heightened, including creativity.[35]

SOLITUDE AND MASTERY

Just as solitude nurtures resilience and creativity, it also enhances our ability to master various skills. In 1993, K. Anders Ericsson famously coined the term "deliberate practice" to describe the focused, solo practice that can lead to mastery of any subject or activity.[36] Ericsson's research found that the top athletes, musicians, chess players, and academics don't excel because they

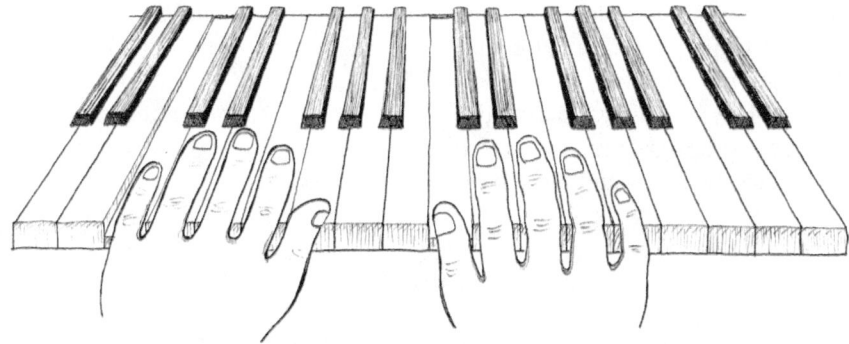

Figure 7.3. Solo practice for approximately twenty minutes a day, followed by constructive feedback from a trusted teacher or advisor, can lead to mastery of any skill. *Kati Haajanen and Esther Aitken.*

are any smarter or more genetically gifted than their competitors (with the exception of genes for height and body size). Rather, gaining independent mastery involves careful reflection on what worked and what didn't work during practice time. Moreover, such practice is best conducted alone.

Think of a piano player focused on scales, a journalist untiringly rewriting the same passage, or a gymnast practicing backflips over and over again on a trampoline. Each one of these examples shows determination to master a concept in order to become better through solo activity. (See figure 7.3)

Here is a simple "deliberate practice" checklist to share with students:

- Set a clear goal for a challenge that pushes you outside of your comfort zone, in that four-to-six range on a scale of one to ten.
- Isolate, or "chunkify," skills and tasks. Break your practice into a series of manageable goals.[37]
- Develop mental representations of superior performance to improve your ability to think about building your potential.
- Practice for approximately fifteen to twenty minutes a day.
- After these periods of solo practice, obtain feedback from a mentor or expert so as to make immediate modifications to your craft.[38]
- Keep track of the stages of your development with a feedback journal.

SOLITUDE IS A MUSCLE

Anyone can strengthen their solitude muscles. It's a matter of practice. Allowing for quiet time to flourish in our schools, free from electronic devices, helps students learn how to be alone with their thoughts. This doesn't mean we value solitude over socializing, but that we seek a balance in our school environments.

We will explore ways to establish quiet spaces at school in the next chapter. Such settings are vital to our ability to cultivate the power of silent reflection in our students—and ourselves.

REFLECTIONS: MICRO-MINDFUL MOMENTS

"Inside myself is a place where I live all alone, and that's where I renew my springs that never dry up."—Pearl Buck

NOISE

1. The bare minimum of time needed to focus and concentrate on a specific task is fifteen minutes. Did you get fifteen minutes of solitude today?
2. Of today's workers, 90 percent say they need quiet, private areas in the workplace. More than 40 percent say they don't have them. Are there any changes that you can make today so that you can be in an optimal environment for independent, creative thinking?
3. The average office worker is interrupted every three minutes. It takes at least twenty-three minutes to refocus after such a distraction. How does your school life compare?

RECHARGING

1. How do you restore your energy after you have been in a situation where you have acted outsideof your comfort zone?
2. What is your favorite "restorative niche?"
3. What helps you to relax and take a break at school? At home?
4. Energy Management Calendar: A daily, weekly, or monthly Energy Management Calendar can help with your recharging needs. Note events/activities that are both non-negotiable and negotiable. In the negotiable category, you can normalize quiet counterpoints to your

days, making the time to sit quietly and let your mind wander or go for a walk outside.

Note that an Energy Management calendar is also beneficial for mixed-personality families, where needs for recharging can be quite divergent. Aim to sit down together and plan for a balance between alone and social times, especially over the weekend or on vacation.

CREATIVITY

1. If you were encouraged to do something creative during "alone time," what would you choose to do? What comes to mind?
2. There are many "brevity" exercises that help build creativity. Try one today: Write for five minutes with your non-dominant hand. Or, try this one: Go for a short walk with only a pen. If something interesting comes to mind, write it on your hand.

MASTERY

1. Reflect on a task you have chosen to master, such as writing, knitting, exercising, baking, mechanical work, or gardening. Identify ways you have improved with practice and three areas you have targeted for improvement in the future.
2. Identify a new skill you wish to acquire. Create a chart showing how you plan to "chunkify" the steps to gain mastery.
3. Select an activity that you have done on a regular basis for many years. As a way to reflect and strengthen your skills in this activity, periodically use a feedback journal to record your strengths, weaknesses, areas for improvement, and personal thoughts.

SOLITUDE IS A MUSCLE

To the annoyance of my family, I often don't reply to texts or messages, but whenever I have the impulse to check in with my phone, I try and check in with myself instead because I think as a society we've lost this quiet moment that was naturally built into our day, whether it was being in an elevator by yourself or with other people, or standing in the grocery line. Now we're all filling that time with checking our phones. And now I think we just have to teach this differently because our brains don't have time to be bored, and therefore we don't have time to be creative and imaginative because we're always receiving information. And if we don't have time to process the information or sit and daydream, we're never going to come up with solutions for the next engineering problem or the next pandemic.—Middle School Library Director[39]

1. How do you handle distractions during the day? How do you help your students to do the same?
2. How can you build your solitude muscle and help your students do the same?

Chapter 8

Quiet Spaces

"When I am alone I can become invisible. I can sit on the top of a dune as motionless as an uprise of weeds, until the foxes run by unconcerned. I can hear the almost unhearable sound of the roses singing."—Mary Oliver

Creating quiet spaces in classrooms, cafeterias, faculty rooms, and on school grounds is a crucial way to rescue solitude in schools where an open floor plan often dominates the architectural landscape. The open-plan learning area, without walls and with tables set in pods, lacks the quiet spaces needed for introverted students to thrive. Without distinct areas for independent work or recharging, the introverts in our school populations are at risk for burnout. Remember that introverts have a heightened sensitivity to social and sensory stimuli, and they need time during a busy school day to restore their nervous systems. There's also a possibility that an overstimulated introvert will retreat, turn inward, or simply shut down.

Research shows that the costs vastly outweigh the benefits of an open-plan classroom for all learners: enhanced opportunities for project-based activities and multidisciplinary work are overshadowed by the inimical effects of noise on learning outcomes. As Amelia Harper reports in "Do Open-Plan Schools Really Work?" (2018), the open-plan design ultimately does not improve educational outcomes for any child, regardless of temperament type, due to the fact that increased noise levels are a learning deterrent. Noise is distracting for all, but especially for introverted learners.[1]

But it's not just the noise that is the problem. Open Education sets the stage for incessant collaboration. Even in today's more traditionally designed schools, where individual classrooms are separated by walls, the main concept behind the Open Education Movement of the 1960s and 1970s still dominates thinking about teaching and learning: everything centers around collaboration.[2] Activities and movement have replaced lectures and independent work. Stillness is a thing of the past.

Rob Cross, Reb Rebele, and Adam Grant affirm in a 2016 *Harvard Business Review* article that we are living in an era of "collaborative overload": they cite a study showing that the average work week is dominated by meetings, calls, and emails, with an astounding 80 percent of time spent on such social activities. Most importantly, their research shows that such social activities sap productivity and lead to disengagement.[3] Every single interview for this book corroborates their findings in schools.

CLASSROOM LAYOUT: PAY ATTENTION TO SOCIAL AND SENSORY STIMULATION

As mentioned previously, a balance between collaboration and independent work creates a learning environment that satisfies all temperament types. The physical plant needs to mirror these dual teaching modalities, and its modification can be an essential way to honor personality diversity in our schools.

Individual mobile desks provide a superior option to the popular collaborative tables in many classrooms in America today. They can be arranged to allow for both independent workspace and teamwork. Extra tables or desks placed along the perimeter of a classroom can create one-on-one and partner-learning areas.

Once the furniture is in place, think about lighting and other features that affect the ambience of the room. Several educators interviewed for this book mentioned that prior to understanding temperament diversity, they used to scold their students if they pulled a hood over their heads during class. It's only in hindsight that they realized that harsh fluorescent overhead lights were painful for their introverted learners. Introverts crave sensory balance with calm and warm influences. Individual lights placed around the room soften the room's character and allow students to control the amount of light they need.

Once the lighting is right, consider other sensory influences that might enhance learning, such as aromatherapy. While the research on aromatherapy is still inconclusive, some studies show that students' concentration may be improved with the use of certain fragrances. For instance, in one study, a simple sniff of a fragrance boosted the speed with which a control group completed a connect-the-dot puzzle.[4]

Since introverts tend to be more sensitive to loud noises than extroverts, it is important to maintain a noise level that is appropriate for all learners. For introverts who are likely to be overstimulated by auditory input, upholstered

Figure 8.1. In order to create a temperament-inclusive classroom, it's critical to set up areas in the room that honor both independent and teamwork. *Kati Haajanen and Esther Aitken.*

pieces, such as soft chairs, rugs, and curtains, can help to absorb sound in the classroom. (See figure 8.1.) Closing the door to the hallway will lessen distracting sights and sounds, and "white noise" headphones can be placed around the room so students can use them at the discretion of the teacher.

Lessening distracting noise can be exceedingly challenging when individual classrooms are separated by flimsy dividers. When one teacher is administering a test in one room, and another teacher with a booming voice is pontificating in an adjoining room, it can be difficult for our introverted students to block out the noise from next door. Psychologist Russell Geen gave math problems to introverts and extroverts, with varying levels of background noise. He found the extroverts did fine when the background noise was loud, but the introverts did much better when the background noise was softer.[5] To prevent this sort of situation from occurring, it is imperative that educators communicate with one another about times in their own classrooms when students need to have silence to focus on their work.

It's not simply social and auditory input that matters when considering the needs of the potentially overstimulated student. Our introverted students will not be in a sweet spot for learning if there is too much visual stimulation in the classroom—anything from posters about all-school events to corkboards announcing the monthly schedule. To paraphrase the words of many introverted students interviewed for this book, "The walls are screaming at me."

Try striking a balance between colorful student work placed on bulletin boards and blank wall spaces. It can be helpful to ask for feedback from students as to whether classroom decorations are enhancing or inhibiting their learning. Often, during one-on-one conversations, introverted students will let educators know that the space does not feel comfortable for their learning style. As one educator affirms, "I had no idea that all of my decorations were distracting for my introverted students. I want all of my students to feel comfortable, safe, and helped."[6]

By contrast, nature can provide a calming visual effect and enhance learning outcomes. Most humans, regardless of temperament type, are biophilic, or genetically predisposed to be drawn to nature. Nature is the environment from which we evolved as humans, and it makes sense that we would, as Harvard biologist E.O. Wilson decreed in the 1980s, love living things and nature. Research by Richard Louv provides examples of the power of nature as a stress-reducer and attention-enhancer. In *Last Child in the Woods*, Louv concludes, based on research from Cornell University's environmental psychologists and Swedish scientists, that a room with a view of nature improves the ability to pay attention.[7] Based on Louv's research, and the pioneering work of Dr. Steven Kettert at Yale University, Bonnie Peters avers in "Biophilic Design in the Learning Environment" (2018) that incorporating aspects of biophilic design in schools can boost attendance, improve test scores, reduce anxiety, and increase focus.[8]

While window views of lush trees or colorful flowers are optimal, a biophilic design does not have to rely on proximity to greenery. This is simply not possible in many of our urban schools. Instead, allow access to natural light—try LED lights that adjust their color over the day to mimic the sky—and use floor and wall coverings made with natural materials, such as wood or stone. Providing classroom workspaces near windows (regardless of the view) and scattering plants around the room can help bring nature indoors.

NOOKS AND BOOKS

It's often hard to get permission to be alone, particularly in schools, where being alone can be seen as being antisocial or a loner. Portable office dividers can create separate spaces around the classroom for students who prefer to work without distraction. Bookshelves and other large furniture in the room may be arranged to form a cozy nook for reading or writing, with control over light and noise.

One introvert-friendly educator took charge of pioneering a quiet-spaces initiative in her school after seeing the positive impact of installing a quiet nook in her classroom. With a keen eye on the working and recharging style of her introverted students, she stocked this quiet corner of her classroom with books, clipboards, markers, puzzles, and mind games. As she states, "In nearly every room in the lower school, there is now a quiet corner—or a cozy corner or a breakout room—or somewhere where kids can go when they're feeling like, 'I need to separate.'"

She continues,

> And it's usually the child who decides, "I need to go work in this quiet place." This is not a punishment place, which I think in years past it always was if someone was misbehaving. Instead this is an inviting place with tactile things, such as glitter jars, so that they could go over and work.[9]

Inviting students to create their own refuge is a way to boost the self-esteem—and creativity—of introverted students. When designing such a creativity challenge, consider some of the following questions: "Where will your quiet space be located? Will there be pictures on the wall or not? Will there be many or just a few objects in your space? Does playing soft music create calmness, or is it best to have total quiet?" Ultimately, these designs can be shared with parents and caregivers if the student grants this permission.

FACULTY SPACES

Introverted faculty and administrators are no different from their students: they need quiet work and recharge space. Teachers who have their own classroom, or share it with another teacher, might consider arranging the room in such a way that allows space to manage their energy according to their own personal needs. If possible, move desks away from the door, so that it is more difficult for others to disrupt thinking with questions or comments during precious moments of preparation time.

At one school in the New England area, a couple of introvert-friendly colleagues gathered to write a grant proposal for creating a quiet space for faculty, a recharge room that tied in with their school's wellness initiative.

> I had often found the study room in the library not being used for its original purpose, and I thought it would be a perfect place to create a recharge room. It's

a small space. The idea was, let's help faculty explore these practices for themselves and do self-care, and that will help them be better teachers. Even if they don't use those practices with their students, they will be in a more grounded, less stressed, less anxious place if they have a space somewhere in the middle of the day where they can go to reset.[10]

For introverted teachers, a classroom workspace, a work cubby in the library, a reading-room table, or a designated quiet space for faculty are all possible options for quiet working and recharging.

SCHOOL BUILDING

If your school is about to receive a makeover, it's the perfect time to meet with planners to try and incorporate an introvert-friendly design into the architectural plan before the work begins. Let's look at how an introvert-friendly educator advocated for introverted students and faculty by discussing plans with architects in advance of the renovation of the school building.

When meeting with the architects, this educator emphasized that enclosed spaces should be created for those who "need to feel a little bit more of that nest-like or that enclosed space that's going to help them feel comfortable." The response of the architects tells it all: they were so moved by her research-based comments that they built little nooks where students could sit alone to complement the large and open spaces. The results: "Our introverted students love them. This architectural space is influenced by not just what works for our more extroverted students, but what also works for our more introverted students, and has led to a better design for everybody."[11]

In the absence of remodeling, it is possible to adapt a current space to allow for quiet work and recharging. The library is an obvious choice for a quiet space. (See figure 8.2.) One librarian interviewed for this book mentioned that she saw her library as a "place of refuge for students who just needed a place that wasn't an assaultive noise or recess . . . students need a place where they can just be away from the hustle and bustle that was elsewhere in the school environment."[12]

Another librarian chose a little room off the main library:

> I decided that it needed to be absolutely silent. You couldn't whisper to people; you couldn't write notes. You were not allowed to interact with another person in that space. People who wanted to read or just have silence had a place they could go, and they knew that somebody was protecting that space.[13]

Many librarians realize that introverts need a quiet recharge space, and the library is often a place that can fulfill that need.

Quiet Spaces　　103

Figure 8.2. The traditional library design, with carrels and signs that prohibit talking, is a haven for introverts, who require minimal social and sensory stimuli in order to do their best work. A temperament-inclusive library today offers both collaborative workspaces and a variety of spaces for those who work best in quiet. *Kati Haajanen and Esther Aitken.*

What about the cafeteria? As mentioned previously, a loud, chaotic lunchroom can be an introvert's nightmare. Lunchtime is often very hectic. For many periods in a row, hundreds of students might cram into what feels like a rectangular box with booming acoustics. What are the alternatives? Ideas include an invitation for children to sit together in another classroom to eat lunch while writing or sitting quietly or an invitation for students to gather in a separate space of the cafeteria for a quiet lunchtime.

One educator initiated a "Peaceful Lunch" movement in her school. It was so successful that she had to ask parents of her New York City public school to monitor the flow of students moving in and out of the dining hall. Out of some nine-hundred-odd students, more than four hundred signed up for "Peaceful Lunch." During each lunch period, approximately twenty kids gathered in a corner of the cafeteria and sat at tables covered in butcher paper with calming glitter jars as centerpieces. Students relished the chance to eat their meal without social expectations for small talk: doodling, drawing, or journaling—or just simply, eating.

If a separate quiet space for eating lunch is not an option, try asking students to create inspiring and attractive table tents to be placed on tables in the cafeteria. These can help spark casual conversation and heighten awareness with a nearly captive audience. Table tents can include inspirational quotes about quiet, solitude, introversion, and reflection. They also can include statistics or myth-busters in the form of "Did you know . . .?" as well as stories about notable individuals from history and pop culture displaying Quiet power, and also more information about the qualities of introversion and benefits of quiet times and spaces.

ON AND OFF SCHOOL GROUNDS

Check the school grounds to see if there are cozy spaces for use by introverts, especially during recess time for younger students. Recess can be overwhelming for introverts, and it is useful for them to know that there is at least one outdoor space provided for quiet time. This can be as simple as a few benches placed along the perimeter of the playground or any other area removed from the center of the activity. Let the students know that these spaces are meant for quiet activities, such as talking with a friend, reading a book, drawing, writing, playing cards, or just thinking.

Some schools have created dedicated outdoor quiet spaces. This can be done on a low budget and can involve students, giving them pride of ownership in a place on their school grounds. At one school in the Midwest, fourth graders redesigned an abandoned garden in the corner of the playground and renamed it the Peace Garden. (See figure 8.3.) As a class, the students created the design—a peace sign shape formed by stone paths—and planted native wildflowers and shrubs within the peace sign. Finally, they placed butterfly-backed benches around the garden and enclosed the space with a picket fence.

As the garden aged, it became known as the quiet area during recess. As the educator who designed the project asserts,

> The kids designed it . . . it became the space where kids could go for quiet recharging during recess . . . if they wanted to read or just walk quietly, or even jump across the rocks, it was a safe space to go. It's more acceptable now to just read during recess or just wander around alone.[14]

Figure 8.3. A Peace Garden can provide a calm space for introverts and extroverts alike. It is an alternative to the busy playground, where loud voices tend to dominate group activities. Time and space permitting, allow students the opportunity to co-create the design of such a quiet zone. *Kati Haajanen and Esther Aitken.*

Today, preschool through high-school students visit the garden to read and write. Faculty and students meet in the garden for conversation and small-group discussions. Individuals come to reflect, read, and hang out. The Peace Garden's quiet personality encourages all to use its welcoming space for recharge and calm.

If a Peace Garden is not an option at your school, try a Saturday morning nature walk. One of the faculty members interviewed for this book was so passionate about helping faculty and students recharge over the weekend that she proposed the idea of a weekend hike at a nature preserve. Her idea is supported by a study by Stephen and Rachel Kaplan, who developed the Attention Restoration Theory, which proposes that exposure to nature is enjoyable and increases focus and concentration levels.[15] As this educator affirms,

> While I don't know if the district will sign off on it, and I don't know if I will be allowed to do it on my own and still invite kids, I am still committed to the idea of meeting at the forest preserve and walking and talking about books. Or simply walking in silence together.[16]

Another idea is to launch a Quiet Power after-school club. Invite students to head outside and just start walking, silently, for about a half-hour or so. Encourage them to give their minds the space needed to reflect and make new connections and to activate their senses during the walk, trying to observe things in new ways. Suggest a technique called "mental contrasting," in which one first imagines a desired goal, and then ponders the obstacles that might impede one's ability to attain the goal. This thought process can be effective in helping to identify areas of passionate interest.[17] Once you are back in the schoolhouse, ask students to document what they were thinking or what they saw along the way through drawing or storytelling: "Did you gravitate toward particular issues, objects, actions, or people? Did you think of things in new ways?"

The benefits of creating opportunities for quiet times inside and outside of the classroom are substantial. In offering such opportunities, even after school and on the weekend, we are demonstrating that we honor and respect all temperament types in our schools. Remember that Duke University's Imke Kirste has shown that two hours of silence per day prompts cell development in the hippocampus, the brain region associated with the formation of memory. During this time, when the brain rests quietly, we allow ourselves to weave into the outside world, to discover where we fit in.[18] Here's to strengthening our solitude muscles in quiet spaces!

REFLECTIONS: MICRO-MINDFUL MOMENTS

"You do not need to leave your room. Remain sitting at your table and listen. Do not even listen, simply wait, be quiet, still and solitary. The world will freely offer itself to you to be unmasked, it has no choice, it will roll in ecstasy at your feet." – Franz Kafka

QUIET CLASSROOM

1. As a teacher, what are your needs and how does the classroom environment fit those needs?
2. In thinking about your own needs, you may want to reach out to one of your parents, or one of your caregivers when you were a child, and ask the following questions:
   a. Did I, as a baby, cry or thrash around when in places where there was a lot of noise?
   b. Did I shut down, cling to a safe person, or have meltdowns in the face of crowds, new people, situations, or busy environments?

3. When designing your classroom, have you included different ways to create quiet spaces? Lighting? Cozy nooks? Furniture placement? Furniture types? Aromatherapy? Plants?

QUIET FACULTY SPACES

We need to provide a place where all students of all temperaments feel valued and safe. And so I look at it from the perspective of the spaces we've provided. I look at it from the perspective of how we talk about children, how we pull them in, engage them in their learning. That all comes down to the space and the feel of the environment for every child, regardless of temperament.[19]

—Elementary School Principal

1. How can you extend this thinking to the care of both introverted and extroverted faculty?
2. How can you adapt this statement to fit your culture and engage colleagues in conversations about quiet spaces?

QUIET SCHOOL BUILDING

1. Does your school have quiet places throughout the building where students can go for recharge time? List some of these places. Are they easily accessible to all students?
2. Do all teachers allow students to use these quiet spaces? Are there spaces available in the school building that can be adapted for a quiet place?
3. What is your lunchroom like? Is it comfortable for all temperament types? If not, what might you change in the lunchroom to make it more comfortable for all?
4. If your school is planning to remodel, is there a group that is aware of including design ideas for temperament-inclusive spaces?

QUIET SCHOOL GROUNDS

1. What are your school grounds like? Are there different types of spaces available for different temperaments? Is there a quiet recharge place? Is there another space for highly stimulating activities?
2. Does your playground have a designated quiet space? If not, where might you create one?

Section IV

LAUNCHING QUIET INITIATIVES

Chapter 9

Call to Action

"No need to hurry. No need to sparkle. No need to be anybody but oneself."—Virginia Woolf

From redesigning leadership programs to facilitating sessions on how to write introvert-inclusive progress reports, the educators profiled in this chapter explain how you can take action to promote a cultural shift in your school. Their experiences will inspire you to think about the best way to launch a Quiet initiative at your organization. Do you want to focus on the way you teach leadership? Design wellness programs? Write anecdotal comments?

Such shifts must begin with raising awareness about behaviors and rituals that are currently embedded in the daily life of your school community. They are often invisible. As Greg Bamford and Carla Silver state in their 2022 NAIS (National Association of Independent Schools) article, "How Schools Talk About and Notice School Culture," cultural change begins with the acknowledgment of biases.[1] Paying attention to what your school culture actually is, and the aspects that may be hurtful to others, is the starting point for any intentional cultural shift.

With this in mind, remember to begin conversations among faculty with these three essential questions (see chapter 1):

- To what extent do we favor bold talkers over reflective listeners as school leaders?
- Do we prize action and stimulation over deliberation and solitude?
- Do we require constant collaboration in open spaces?

Shadowing students can be a useful way to investigate the levels of social and sensory stimulation required during the school day: the length of time provided for passing between classes, the frequency of classroom discussions, and the brightness of lights in classrooms.

When a Quiet initiative is launched in a deliberate manner, the overall result can be a school that is characterized by a temperament-inclusive culture in which everyone is recognized for their potential to lead in authentic ways. The ultimate goal is to unite entire school communities—administrators, educators, students, and parents—around the common goal of harnessing the strengths of both introverts and extroverts.[2]

LEADERSHIP PROGRAM APPROACH

Cultivating expansive approaches to the election—or selection—of student leaders enables introverts as well as extroverts to develop and apply leadership skills. (See figure 9.1.) In this first story, a middle school leadership program director shares that her Quiet leadership initiative stemmed from a one-size-fits-all definition of leadership at her school:

> We have leadership opportunities without teaching kids how to be leaders. It's a popularity contest where kids are expected to run the show—to be chiefs. They all have to learn how to be chiefs and followers, too. With our middle schoolers, we had a retreat at the beginning of school and delved deeply into leadership. It was important for them to understand what kind of a leader they are, and to know that it is okay if they aren't the ones doing all the talking; there are lots of different ways to lead.[3]

Under this administrator's guidance, the school replaced the class officer election system with a new model for seventh and eighth graders: an application process and a ten-minute interview. Based on the interviews, the faculty selected fifteen students to be the middle-school class officers. She summarizes: "While not as many students had the opportunity for leadership in one academic year, they were positive role models for others, leading by example, whether that was leading by listening, leading by coordinating, or another leadership strength."[4]

In a similar way, an elementary school principal asked for recommendations from faculty to create an Advisory Council of fourth- and fifth-grade students—but only *after* students filled out an "interest form." That form included questions about primary areas of interest, self-defined strengths, and ways to contribute to the group: "The faculty were asked to fill the twelve-member Advisory Council with a blend of different temperaments. One of our tenets was that every voice in the council needs to be heard at each meeting. We focused on allowing for sharing and reflection in both small groups and whole groups, so that the students could play to their strengths."[5]

Call to Action

Figure 9.1. Some students are more naturally gifted as speakers, and others as listeners. Broadening opportunities for leadership in our schools enables both introverts and extroverts to take the stage to share their passion and mission with their peers. *Kati Haajanen and Esther Aitken.*

How can you empower students of all ages to know that they can be both an introvert and a leader?

DIVERSITY, EQUITY, AND INCLUSION APPROACH

In this next story, a DEI director, after repeatedly witnessing extrovert-dominated faculty meetings, knew that her school needed to work on the issue of personality inclusivity. As she says,

> Often, just a few people were the ones who were speaking. And so, it became clear that we needed something that would help us create a feeling of community, because when we came together as a group, you couldn't really tell since only certain people were talking. I think that in that division meeting space—that's an hour and a half, once a week—people knew that there was a more effective way to use that time.[6]

Her wise words of advice:

Take note of systemic issues that are impacting students and faculty in a negative way . . . Diversity actually means all different kinds of identities that people have—and reminding people that they have so many different ones in their being. And that was how we opened it up so that people could think about personality in addition to race and gender.[7]

What can you do from an institutional perspective to confront extrovert bias in your school culture—as opposed to solving just one person's problem or issue?

WELLNESS APPROACH

This story from a lower school teacher suggests that an effective way to launch a Quiet initiative is to link it with a school-wide health and wellness movement:

Quiet was pushed forward through an overall wellness program that we have now instituted at our school . . . so that it's not so much a Quiet movement but a health movement, which definitely includes Quiet. At the beginning of the year, we're given two-hundred dollars to spend as "health dollars," and it can be for a massage, it can be for a meditation program, or for workout equipment. It really can be for anything. So, the movement involves reaching out to meet people's individual health needs.

What might you do with two hundred dollars for your mental, physical, and emotional health? If you don't have access to this sort of resource, how might you teach others that overstimulation is a health and wellness concern?

PROGRESS REPORTS APPROACH

The following story reveals how one faculty member encouraged his colleagues to incorporate introvert-inclusive language when writing narrative reports. To paraphrase many of the interviewees for this book, the "tyranny of the verbal participation grade" leads to a Quiet initiative: "In narrative comments, I noticed that we used expressions like, 'Even though you never participate in class,' or 'I'd like to see you raise your hand more,' or 'When you work with a group, you need to be more of a leader.'"[8]

This educator worked with his faculty to highlight the strengths of introverts in written comments:

Quiet anchor comments are simple, and give us some sentence starters. With this language and knowledge, we are able to comment not just on the fact that someone raises their hand all the time in class, but that part of their participation might be staying after class and asking a question one-on-one or sending the teacher an email to ask a clarifying question.[9]

Here are a few "quiet anchor comments" for inspiration (see chapter 5):

- Harper is attentive to details, which serves him well during long-term projects.
- Robin cares deeply about forging meaningful relationships, and she is a sought-after partner in class.
- Stephan is deliberate in his thoughts and actions, takes time to offer thoughtful reflections, and perseveres in his work.
- Georgina is an innovative thinker who thrives during independent tasks.
- Zamir leads by listening to others, empowering them to do the same.

Which of these "quiet anchor comments" might you share with your faculty? Do you have others to set the stage for temperament-inclusivity in interactions with parents and caregivers? (See figure 9.2.)

Figure 9.2. Quiet anchor comments set the stage for temperament-inclusivity in our schools, and they can be a highly effective tool in encouraging introverted students to both own their strengths and flex their style in the service of a core personal project. **Kati Haajanen and Esther Aitken.**

ONE-ON-ONE COACHING APPROACH

When educators truly get to know their students, they will be able to see the manifestation of leadership in each individual. The sensitivity of an educator to a student's personality style can unlock that student's leadership potential, and it's often a one-on-one approach that sets the introverted student at ease.

One-on-one sessions can be effective when they include the mutual sharing of vulnerability stories. For example, an educator may share a time when she froze during a piano recital in her junior year of high school, and then showed up a few weeks later to play the same piece at the next recital. Such modeling of a vulnerability story helps students share times when they have stretched outside their comfort zones, faced challenges, and learned from their mistakes.

If you have time for one-on-one meetings with your students, what is your "signature vulnerability story" that you might want to share with them?

QUIET AMBASSADORS

The time is right to nurture the next generation to be self-aware, empathetic, and humble leaders who are adept at actualizing the potential of team members to devise creative solutions to complex, adaptive challenges. May this book help you to open doors for quietly confident and compassionate leaders and foster cultures of belonging at your school or organization. Think of yourselves as Quiet Ambassadors, engaging in personal journeys of self-discovery for the benefit of all.

Acknowledgments

This book is designed to transform communities, and, as such, it is an extension of the work that I have done with one of the most inspirational thought leaders of the twenty-first century, Susan Cain. I will never forget the day in 2015 when she dubbed me a "Quiet Revolutionary" and offered me a position as director of education at her organization, Quiet Revolution. Her book, *Quiet: The Power of Introverts in a World That Can't Stop Talking*, had changed my life, and I was honored by the opportunity to create a national professional development program based on the main tenets of *Quiet*.

It is in the spirit of accelerating and expanding the Quiet movement that I write this book for all of my colleagues in the field of education who wake up day after day to guide the next generation to be empathetic, resilient, and compassionate leaders. I know just how challenging it is to show up at school every day; I also know how exhilarating it can be to work with kids on a daily basis.

I have taken much inspiration from many other thought leaders in the various fields of diversity and inclusion, introversion/extroversion, history, leadership, mindfulness, resilience, and solitude, including Matthew Barzun, Beth L. Buelow, JoAnn Deak, Amy Edmonson, Adam Grant, Laurie Helgoe, Tony Judt, Jennifer Kahnweiler, Scott Barry Kaufman, Jessica Lahey, Marti Olsen Laney, Brian Little, Irshad Manji, Matthew Pollard, Sheryl Sandberg, Simon Sinek, Robert Thurman, and Justin Zorn and Leigh Marz. Your books are filled with my Post-it notes, and to this day, they sit on my shelf as sources of creativity and knowledge.

I am particularly grateful for the educators who joined our original cohort at Quiet Revolution as Quiet Ambassadors: Tracy Ainsworth, Lisa Alberti, Susan Abramson, Joseph Algarant, Jacki Bissu, Kelvina Butcher, Andy Callender, Karin Carnegie, Timothy Coyne, Wendy Demming, Lee Dieck,

James Donnel, Susan Doyle, Lorri Hamilton Durbin, Monica Edinger, Tracy Fedonchik, Alan Fegley, Ben Fleisher, Jeannie Forrest, Lisa Green, Melanie Greenup, Patricia Hans, Beth Hartley, Kelly Hurst, Joe Jividen, Russell Joy, Jessica Kelly, Kirsten Kinney, Emily Kolatch, Terry Lee, Ivy Leibowitz, Kim Lewis, Malia McClurg, Vanesha McGee, Emily Miner, Rori Minissale, Rachel Mumford, Marie Murphy, Sara Obarow, Craig Parkinson, Erin Pawlak, Kimberly Peeples, Tracy Poverstein, Peggy Procter, Camar Robinson, Amanda Rose, Dawn Rosevear, Alyse Ruiz, Eva Seligman, Heather Sherman, Lily Shum, Joan Slattery, Emmett Smith, Linda Speckhals, Charlotte Stiverson, Khalid Sutton, Gillian Todd, Heather Way, Michele Wright, Mary Yockey, and Jennifer Zanoria.

I am also thankful for the stunning work from all members of the Quiet Schools Network team, including Nidhi Berry, Kate Earle, Michael Glass, and Homa Tavangar. And to our fearless facilitators during that first year: Nicole Cohen, Erica Corbin, Cathy Cramer, Heather Durosko, Daisy Swan, and Michelle Wonsley.

I have been fortunate to reconnect with many Quiet Ambassadors, as well as their friends and colleagues, for interviews about their experiences with introverted students at their respective schools. I am grateful to everyone with whom I spoke, and I want to highlight the names of the individuals cited in this book: Britt Anderson, Derek Boonisar, Janetta Davis, Ted Fish, Jessica Fries-Gaither, Carrie Green, Betsy Gugle, Patty Hans, Aniele Hawking, Sam Kane, Ally Leonard, Joanne Magee, Sean Patrick McGowan, Linda Resch, Annie Ruefle, Casey Selover, Robin Smith, Charlotte Stiverson, Jen Waldeck, Matthew Williams, Kim Rice Wilson, and Mary Yockey.

There were many friends who cheered me on through the pandemic and beyond, whose words of wisdom and encouragement brought me back to the manuscript day after day. I want to begin with my colleagues at the Gardner Carney Leadership Institute, many of whom have been a steady force in my life since I first attended the gcLi Leadership Lab in 2012. Jeremy LaCasse, my colleague in blazing new trails in leadership education, is always available for a chat about ideas and dreams. Dr. JoAnn Deak inspired me to believe in myself and my ability to transform schools with innovative leadership programming. I also want to recognize Emily Ihrke for her support of my leadership work with students and faculty, Mike Pardee for encouraging me to be a "rock star," and Katherine Berdy for her enthusiasm about the future of leadership education.

Special thanks goes to my colleagues and friends who have supported me over the years, from near and far: Kitty Gordan and Dorothy Hutcheson for their mentorship when I was a department chair at an independent school in New York City; Mary Jean McCarthy for her thoughtful conversations about innovative approaches in the field of Quiet pedagogy; Amanda Allan for her sisterly care and never-ending support; Chloe Porter for encouraging me to return to India for her yoga retreat at a time when I needed it most; Rob Roznowski and Carolyn Conover for the productive time we spent together co-creating *The Introverted Actor: Practical Approaches*; Haiyun Lu for her profound understanding of me as a Quiet leader, and also Ernest Stambouly and Steve Smith for supporting me as an executive coach.

This publication would not have been possible without the expertise of those who have donated their time and talents in their respective fields of editing and illustrating. Thank you Cynthia Bushmann for reading drafts and gently nudging me to shift a word here or there, and Esther Aitken and Kati Haajanen, for your expressive illustrations.

Most of all, I thank my family. My two beloved and accomplished children, Emily and Jeremy, never cease to light up each and every day of my life with stories of their own adventures. Their loving words energize me for the next steps in my own creative journey, and I cherish every conversation we have about careers, families, and living a good life. My stepchildren, Megan, Justine, and Patrick, continually remind me that travel and humor are key ingredients to a life well-lived. My brother Mark guides me in navigating life's challenges with an optimistic spirit. My mother-in-law, Anne, was a revered high-school math teacher who was always eager to discuss best practices in education.

To my dear husband, Sean: *merci mille fois* for believing in me and making the time and space in our lives to allow me to focus on writing this book. Your hours of providing feedback on my drafts, shopping for supplies, and walking our dog Coco when I was "just about to finish up," and assuring me that "I can do it!" were, and will forever be, countless and invaluable.

And finally, to my innovative and intrepid parents, Elizabeth *the artist* and Ray *the scientist*: thank you for demonstrating what it means to live each day to the fullest, to take risks, and to follow your passions. I know that I have your eternal love, and it is to both of you that I dedicate this book.

Notes

CHAPTER 1

1. Michael Godsey, "Teaching: Not for Introverts," *The Atlantic, Atlantic Media Company*, 21, last modified January 25, 2016, https://www.theatlantic.com/education/archive/2016/01/why-introverted-teachers-are-burning-out/425151/.

2. Susan Cain, *Quiet: The Power of Introverts in a World That Can't Stop Talking* (New York: Crown Publishing Group, 2012), 271–285.

3. Warren I. Susman, *Culture as History: The Transformation of American Society in the Twentieth Century* (Washington, DC: Smithsonian Inst. Press, 2003).

4. Joanne Magee, Interview by Heidi Kasevich, April 29, 2019.

5. C.G. Jung, *Psychological Types* (Zurich: Rascher Verlag, 1921), 330–337 quoted in Cain, *Quiet: The Power of Introverts*, 10.

6. Merve Emre, *The Personality Brokers: the Strange History of Myers-Briggs and the Birth of Personality Testing* (Toronto: Vintage Canada, 2019), 33–39.

7. Sophia Dembling, *The Introverts Way: Living a Quiet Life in a Noisy World* (New York: Penguin Group, 2012), 5–9.

8. Marti Olsen Laney, Psy.D., *The Hidden Gifts of the Introverted Child—Helping Your Child Thrive in an Extroverted World* (New York: Workman Publishing Company, Inc., 2005), 8–9.

9. Bernard Davidson, Ralph A. Gillies, and Allen L. Pelletier, "Introversion and Medical Student Education: Challenges for Both Students and Educators," *Teaching and Learning in Medicine* 27, no. 1 (February 2015): 99–104. https://doi.org/10.1080/10401334.2014.979183.

10. Cain, *Quiet: The Power of Introverts*, 29.

11. Cain, *Quiet: The Power of Introverts*, 31, and Susan Cain, "Shyness: An Evolutionary Tactic?" *The New York Times,* June 25, 2011, https://www.nytimes.com/2011/06/26/opinion/sunday/26shyness.html.

12. Kelly Wickam Hurst, "Quiet Black Girls—And How We Fail Them," *Quiet Revolution*, https://quietrev.com/quiet-black-girls-and-how-we-fail-them/.

13. Hurst, "Quiet Black Girls."
14. M. R. Banaji and Anthony G. Greenwald, *Blindspot: Hidden Biases of Good People* (New York: Bantam Books, 2016), 9.
15. Walter Lippman, *Public Opinion* (New York: Penguin Books, 1922), 73.
16. Monica Fuglei, "Unconscious Discrimination: How to Defeat Four Hidden Teacher Biases," *Resilient Educator*, September 7, 2018, https://education.cu-portland.edu/blog/classroom-resources/unconscious-discrimination-avoiding-teacher-biases.
17. Ellen Hendriksen, "The 4 Differences Between Introversion and Social Anxiety," *Quiet Revolution*, May 20, 2016, https://www.quietrev.com/the-4-differences-between-introversion-and-social-anxiety/.
18. Laurie Helgoe, "Revenge of the Introvert," *Psychology Today,* September 1, 2010, https://www.psychologytoday.com/us/articles/201009/revenge-the-introvert.
19. Derek Boonisar, Interview by Heidi Kasevich, June 26, 2020.
20. Cain, *Quiet: The Power of Introverts*, 4.
21. Margarita Tartakovsky, "Seven Persistent Myths about Introverts and Extroverts," *Psych Central*, September 11, 2013, https://psychcentral.com/blog/7-persistent-myths-about-introverts-extroverts#1.
22. Annie Ruefle, Interview by Heidi Kasevich, August 14, 2020.
23. Patty Hans, Interview by Heidi Kasevich, June 18, 2020.
24. Ted Fish, Interview by Heidi Kasevich, June 18, 2020.
25. Joanne Magee, Interview by Heidi Kasevich, April 29, 2019.
26. Britt Anderson, Interview by Heidi Kasevich, June 12, 2020.
27. Charlotte Stiverson, Conversation with Heidi Kasevich, May 10, 2023.
28. Sean Patrick McGowan, Interview by Heidi Kasevich, April 13, 2019.
29. Banaji and Greenwald, *Blindspot: Hidden Biases of Good People*, 15.

CHAPTER 2

1. Ted Fish, Interview by Heidi Kasevich, June 18, 2020.
2. Carrie Green, Interview by Heidi Kasevich, August 27, 2020.
3. Jessica Fries-Gaither, Interview by Heidi Kasevich, August 5, 2020.
4. Adam Grant, "Say Goodbye to MBTI, the Fad That Won't Die," *LinkedIn*, accessed November 21, 2019, https://www.linkedin.com/pulse/20130917155206-69244073-say-goodbye-to-mbti-the-fad-that-won-t-die.
5. Scott Barry Kaufman, "How to Change Your Personality," *The Atlantic. Atlantic Media Company,* last modified July 30, 2016, https://www.theatlantic.com/health/archive/2016/07/can-personality-be-changed/492956/; Scott Barry Kaufman, "The Real Science of Introversion (and the Rest of Personality)," *Scientific American Blog Network*, last modified December 7, 2015, https://blogs.scientificamerican.com/beautiful-minds/the-real-science-of-introversion-and-the-rest-of-personality/.
6. Sybil B. G. Eysenck and H. J. Eysenck, "Salivary Response to Lemon Juice as a Measure of Introversion," *Perceptual and Motor Skills* 24, no. 3 (1967): 1047–1053.

7. Jerome Kagan and Nancy C. Snidman. *The Long Shadow of Temperament* (Cambridge, MA: Harvard University Press 2009), 2–28.

8. Carl E. Schwartz, Nancy C. Snidman, and Jerome Kagan, "Adolescent Social Anxiety as an Outcome of Inhibited Temperament in Childhood," *Journal of the American Academy of Child & Adolescent Psychiatry* 38, no. 8 (1999): 1008–15, https://doi.org/10.1097/00004583-199908000-00017.

9. Susan Cain, "The Long Runway," *Quiet, the Power of Introverts Podcast/Panoply/Quiet Revolution*, February 3, 2016, https://susancain.net/susan-cain-quiet-podcast/.

10. Marianne Szegedy-Maszak, "As Noise Rises, so Do the Dangers," *Los Angeles Times*, last modified November 28, 2005, https://www.latimes.com/archives/la-xpm-2005-nov-28-he-noise28-story.html.

11. Jennifer Granneman, "Why Introverts and Extroverts Are Different: The Science," *Quiet Revolution*, last modified December 21, 2015, https://www.quietrev.com/why-introverts-and-extroverts-are-different-the-science/.

12. Michael C. Ashton, Kibeom Lee, and Sampo V. Paunonen, "What Is the Central Feature of Extraversion? Social Attention versus Reward Sensitivity," *Journal of Personality and Social Psychology* 83, no. 1 (2002): 245–252, https://doi.org/10.1037/0022-3514.83.1.245.

13. Scott Barry Kaufman, "Will the Real Introverts Please Stand Up?," *Scientific American Blog Network*, last modified June 9, 2014, https://blogs.scientificamerican.com/beautiful-minds/will-the-real-introverts-please-stand-up?.

14. Marti Olsen Laney, *The Introvert Advantage* (New York: Workman Publishing 2002), 71–86.

15. Adam Grant, "5 Myths About Introverts and Extroverts," *Quiet Revolution*, September 23, 2015, https://www.quietrev.com/5-myths-about-introverts-and-extroverts/.

16. There are many Introvert/Extrovert assessments available, including ones by Myers-Briggs, Susan Cain, Introvert Dear, VeryWell Mind, and Marti Olsen Laney. This one represents a combination of many assessments and is unique to this book.

17. The original "Who am I Cube?" was created by Charlotte Stiverson. Charlotte Stiverson, Conversation with Heidi Kasevich, February 15, 2023.

18. Susan Cain, Quiet Revolution Study, 2014. https://quietrev.com/resources-for-schools/.

19. Robert Greenleaf, *The Servant as Leader* (New Jersey: The Greenleaf Center for Servant Leadership, 2015), 30–35.

20. Pelin Kesebir and Selin Kesebir, "The Cultural Salience of Moral Character and Virtue Declined in Twentieth Century America," *Journal of Positive Psychology*, November, 2012. https://doi.org/10.1080/17439760.2016.1167940.

21. Jennifer Cole Wright, "The Psychological Significance of Humility," *Journal of Positive Psychology*, April 22, 2016, https://doi.org/10.1080/17439760.2016.1167940.

22. "Humility," *Values in Action Institute on Character,* https://www.viacharacter.org/character-strengths/humility.

23. Bradley Owens and David Hekman, "Modeling How to Grow: An Inductive Examination of Humble Leader Behavior, Contingencies, and Outcomes," *Academy*

of Management Journal, 55, no. 4 (April 2012), https://journals.aom.org/doi/abs/10.5465/amj.2010.044.

24. Jeanine Prime and Elizabeth Salib, "The Best Leaders Are Humble Leaders," *Harvard Business Review,* last modified May 12, 2014, https://hbr.org/2014/05/the-best-leaders-are-humble-leaders.

25. Vicki Zakrzewski, "How to Cultivate Humble Leadership," *Greater Good Magazine,* last modified February 2016, https://greatergood.berkeley.edu/article/item/how_to_cultivate_humble_leadership.

26. Tenelle Porter, "The Benefits of Admitting When You Don't Know," *Greater Good Magazine,* July 16, 2018, https://greatergood.berkeley.edu/article/item/the_benefits_of_admitting_when_you_dont_know.

27. Adam M. Grant, Francesca Gino, and David A. Hofmann, "The Hidden Advantages of Quiet Bosses," *Harvard Business Review*, December 2010, https://hbr.org/2010/12/the-hidden-advantages-of-quiet-bosses.

28. "Perspective," *Values in Action Institute on Character,* https://www.viacharacter.org/character-strengths/perspective.

29. "Perspective," *Values in Action Institute on Character.*

30. Robin Smith, Interview by Heidi Kasevich, September 16, 2020.

31. Andy Hinds, "The World's Richest Introvert," *Quiet Revolution*, August 6, 2023, https://quietrev.com/warren-buffett/.

32. Arthur C. Brooks, "How the Modern World Made Cowards of Us All," *The New York Times*, July 21, 2017, https://www.nytimes.com/2017/07/21/opinion/how-the-modern-world-made-cowards-of-us-all.html?searchResultPosition=1.

33. Ted Fish, Interview by Heidi Kasevich, June 18, 2020.

34. Miranda Johnson, "The Qualities of an Introverted Leader," *Quiet Diarist—Quiet Revolution,* https://quietrev.com/quiet_diaries/the-qualities-of-an-introverted-leader/.

CHAPTER 3

1. Brain Little quoted in Adam Grant, "The Science of Personality and the Art of Well-being with Brian Little," *WorkLife with Adam Grant*, TED Original Podcast, July 10, 2023, https://www.ted.com/podcasts/worklife.

2. Brian R. Little, "Personal Projects and Free Traits: Personality and Motivation Reconsidered," October 24, 2011, https://www.brianrlittle.com/articles/personal-projects-and-free-traits/.

3. Brian R. Little, "How Your To-Do List Shapes Your Personality—and How to Use It to Remake Who You Are," *Ideas.Ted.Com*, August 15, 2017, https://ideas.ted.com/how-our-projects-shape-our-personalities-and-how-we-can-use-them-to-remake-who-we-are/.

4. Janet Polivy and C. Peter Herman, "Dieting and Binging: A Causal Analysis," *American Psychologist* 40, no. 2 (1985): 193–201. https://doi.org/10.1037/0003-066x.40.2.193.

5. Susan Cain, *Quiet: The Power of Introverts in a World That Can't Stop Talking* (New York: Crown Publishing Group, 2012), 118.
6. The Stretch Meter was developed in collaboration with Charlotte Stiverson.
7. Jessica Fries-Gaither, Interview by Heidi Kasevich, August 5, 2020.
8. Jessica Fries-Gaither, Interview by Heidi Kasevich, August 5, 2020.
9. Robin Smith, Interview by Heidi Kasevich, September 16, 2020.
10. Robin Smith, Interview by Heidi Kasevich, September 16, 2020.
11. Brian Little, "Acting Out of Character in the Immortal Profession: Toward a Free Trait Agreement," *Academic Matters*, April- May 2010, https://www.brianrlittle.com/articles/acting-out-of-character-in-the-immortal-profession-toward-a-free-trait-agreement/?doing_wp_cron=1714173623.9683148860931396484375.
12. Ted Fish, Interview by Heidi Kasevich, June 18, 2020.

CHAPTER 4

1. Casey Selover, Interview by Heidi Kasevich, August 21, 2020.
2. Casey Selover, Interview by Heidi Kasevich, August 21, 2020.
3. Aniele Hawkins, Interview by Heidi Kasevich, August 21, 2020.
4. Jack Zenger and Joseph Folkman, "What Great Listeners Actually Do," *Harvard Business Review*, July 14, 2016, https://hbr.org/2016/07/what-great-listeners-actually-do.
5. Amy Cuddy, *Presence: Bringing Your Boldest Self to Your Biggest Challenges* (Boston, MA: Little, Brown and Company, 2015), 81.
6. Deborah Grunefeld, "Power and Influence," *VMware Women's Leadership Innovation Lab*, https://womensleadership.stanford.edu/resources/voice-influence/power-influence.
7. Patti Wood, "The Gold Standard of Listening," https://www.pattiwood.net/article.asp?PageID=2323.
8. Mike Bechtle, "Are you Talking to an Extrovert or an Introvert?" https://www.mikebechtle.com/are-you-talking-to-an-extrovert-or-an-introvert/.
9. The author developed the original Quiet Engagement Rubric for Quiet Revolution in 2017. https://quietrev.com/wp-content/uploads/2018/11/RS-Quiet-Student-Engagement-Rubric.pdf.
10. Jessica Fries-Gaither, Interview by Heidi Kasevich, August 5, 2020.
11. Jen Waldeck, Interview by Heidi Kasevich, June 19, 2020.
12. Aniele Hawkins, Interview by Heidi Kasevich, August 21, 2020.
13. Derek Boonisar, Interview by Heidi Kasevich, June 26, 2020.
14. Aniele Hawkins, Interview by Heidi Kasevich, August 21, 2020.
15. Casey Selover, Interview by Heidi Kasevich, August 21, 2020.
16. Jessica Fries-Gaither, Interview by Heidi Kasevich, August 5, 2020.
17. Ted Fish, Interview by Heidi Kasevich, June 18, 2020.

CHAPTER 5

1. Susan Cain, "The Long Runway," *Quiet, the Power of Introverts Podcast/Panoply/Quiet Revolution*, February 3, 2016, https://susancain.net/susan-cain-quiet-podcast/.
2. Patty Hans, Interview by Heidi Kasevich, August 5, 2020.
3. Sam Kane, Interview by Heidi Kasevich, June 29, 2020.
4. Sam Kane, Interview by Heidi Kasevich, June 29, 2020.
5. Patricia A. Jennings, *Mindfulness for Teachers: Simple Skill for Peace and Productivity in the Classroom* (New York, W & W Norton and Company, 2015), 155.
6. Judith L. Shrum, "Wait Time and Student Performance Level in Second Language Classrooms," *The Journal of Classroom Interaction* 20, no. 1 (1984): 29–35, http://www.jstor.org/stable/43997866.
7. Aniele Hawkins, Interview by Heidi Kasevich, August 21, 2020.
8. Mary Budd Rowe, "Wait Time and Rewards as Instructional Variables," *ERIC Clearinghouse for Social Studies/Social Science Education*, April 1972, https://archive.org/details/ERIC_ED061103.
9. Judy Lightner and LeighAnn Tomaswick, "Teaching Tools in a Flash, Active Learning—Think, Pair, Share," *Kent State University, Center for Teaching and Learning,* February 1, 2017, https://www-s3-live.kent.edu/s3fs-root/s3fs-public/file/Teaching%20Tools%20in%20A%20Flash%20-%20Think%2C%20Pair%2C%20Share%20%20-%20Final.pdf?VersionId=I1tG2t8a9oi_cwhe_4U5V3u0Qc7emXPU.
10. Lightner and Tomaswick, "Think, Pair, Share."
11. Hanisha Besant, "The Journey of Brainstorming," *Journal of Transformational Innovation* 2, no. 1 (Summer 2016), https://www.academia.edu/65349381/The_Journey_of_Brainstorming.
12. Leigh Thompson, "How Brainwriting Can Get Better Ideas Out of Your Team," *Harvard Business Review*, May 16, 2017, https://hbr.org/sponsored/2017/05/how-brainwriting-can-get-better-ideas-out-of-your-team.
13. "Groupthink," *Psychology Today Staff*, November 1971, https://www.psychologytoday.com/us/basics/groupthink.
14. Gregory S. Berns, Jonathan Chappelow, Caroline F. Zink, Giuseppe Pagnoni, Megan E. Martin-Skurski, and Jim Richards, "Neurobiological Correlates of Social Conformity and Independence During Mental Rotation," *Society of Biological Psychiatry*, 2005, https://www.ccnl.emory.edu/greg/Berns%20Conformity%20final%20printed.pdf.
15. Adam Grant, "Why Brainstorming Doesn't Work," *Time*, October 24, 2023, https://time.com/6327515/brainstorming-doesnt-work-essay/.
16. Rick Howard and Maeve McKillen, "Extraversion and Performance in the Perceptual Maze Test," *Personality and Individual Differences* 11, no. 4 (1990): 391–396, https://doi.org/10.1016/0191-8869(90)90,221-C.
17. Janetta Davis, Interview by Heidi Kasevich, August 4, 2020.

CHAPTER 6

1. Olaf Jorgenson, "The Parent-School Partnership: Optimizing Relationships and Building Understanding," *NAIS*, January 31, 2023, https://www.nais.org/learn/independent-ideas/january-2023/the-parent-school-partnership-optimizing-relationships-and-building-understanding/?utm_source=bn&utm_medium=email&utm_campaign=mc&utm_content=ltc.
2. Marti Olsen Laney, Psy.D., *The Hidden Gifts of the Introverted Child—Helping Your Child Thrive in an Extroverted World* (New York: Workman Publishing Company, Inc., 2005), 96–106.
3. Christine Fonseca, *Quiet Kids—Help Your Introverted Child Succeed in an Extroverted World* (Waco, TX: Prufrock Press Inc., 2014), 55–59.
4. Kim Wilson, Interview by Heidi Kasevich, August 11, 2020.
5. Betsy Gugle, Interview by Heidi Kasevich, June 9, 2020.
6. A.A. Milne, *The Complete Tales of Winnie-the-Pooh* (New York: Dutton Children's Books, 1994), 256–272.
7. Roald Dahl, *Matilda* (New York: Viking, 1988), 66.
8. J.R.R. Tolkien, *The Hobbit* (New York: Ballantine Books, Inc., 1966).
9. Charlotte Stiverson, Conversation with Heidi Kasevich, July 2023.
10. Charlotte Stiverson, Interview by Heidi Kasevich, June 10, 2020.

CHAPTER 7

1. Nadia Whitehead, "People Would Rather be Electrically Shocked than Left Alone with Their Thoughts," *Science*, July 3, 2014, https://www.science.org/doi/10.1126/science.1250830.
2. Justin Zorn and Leigh Marz, "How to Build a Culture that Honors Quiet Time," *Harvard Business Review*, May 24, 2022, https://hbr.org/2022/05/how-to-build-a-culture-that-honors-quiet-time.
3. Justin Zorn and Leigh Marz, *Golden: The Power of Silence in a World of Noise* (New York: HarperCollins, 2022), 11.
4. Zorn and Marz, "How to Build a Culture."
5. Lydia Saad, "Americans Have Close But Wary Bond With Their Smartphone," *Gallup*, June 20, 2022, https://news.gallup.com/poll/393785/americans-close-wary-bond-smartphone.aspx.
6. Melissa Dahl, "How Prolonged Exposure to Sweet, Blessed Silence Benefits the Brain," *New York*, July 8, 2016, https://www.thecut.com/2016/07/scientists-are-discovering-the-neural-benefits-of-silence.html.
7. Marianne Szegedy-Maszak, "As Noise Rises, So Do the Dangers," *Los Angeles Times*, November 28, 2005, https://www.latimes.com/archives/la-xpm-2005-nov-28-he-noise28-story.html.
8. Rance, G., R.C. Dowell, and D. Tomlin. "The Effect of the Classroom Environment on Literacy Development," *NPJ Science of Learning* 8, no. 9 (2023), https://doi.org/10.1038/s41539-023-00157-y.

9. Ethan Cross, *Chatter: The Voice in our Head, Why It Matters, and How to Harness It* (New York: Crown, 2021), 29.

10. Margot Wielgus, Thomas Böhm, and Günter Figal, "Solitude & Thinking: Henry David Thoreau," in *Anthropologie Der Theorie*, ed. Thomas Jürgasch and Tobias Keiling (Mohr Siebeck GmbH and Co. KG, 2017), 209–224, http://www.jstor.org/stable/j.ctvrs90hh.12.

11. Diana Senechal, *Republic of Noise: The Loss of Solitude in Schools and Culture* (Lanham, MD: Rowman & Littlefield, 2012), 23.

12. Daniel Gross, "This Is Your Brain on Silence," *Nautilus*, July 13, 2014, https://nautil.us/this-is-your-brain-on-silence-235023/.

13. Reed W. Larson, "The Emergence of Solitude as a Constructive Domain of Experience in Early Adolescence," *Society for Research in Child Development*, June 30, 2006, https://doi.org/10.1111/j.1467–8624.1997.tb01927.x.

14. Gross, "This is Your Brain on Silence."

15. Gross, "This is Your Brain on Silence."

16. Brian R. Little, *Me, Myself and Us*, (New York: PublicAffairs, 2014), 63.

17. Brian R. Little, "Personal Projects and Free Traits: Personality and Motivation Reconsidered," *Social and Personality Psychology Compass* 2, no. 3 (2008): 1235–1254, https://doi.org/10.1111/j.1751-9004.2008.00106.x.

18. Charlotte Stiverson, Interview by Heidi Kasevich, June 10, 2020.

19. Jen Waldeck, Interview by Heidi Kasevich, June 19, 2020.

20. Sam Kane, Interview by Heidi Kasevich, June 29, 2020.

21. Jen Waldeck, Interview by Heidi Kasevich, June 19, 2020.

22. Linda Resch, Interview by Heidi Kasevich, July 29, 2020.

23. Linda Resch, Interview by Heidi Kasevich, July 29, 2020.

24. Janetta Davis, Interview by Heidi Kasevich, August 4, 2020.

25. Janetta Davis, Interview by Heidi Kasevich, August 4, 2020.

26. Shawn Achor and Michelle Gielen, "Resilience Is About How You Recharge, Not How You Endure," *Harvard Business Review*, June 24, 2016, https://hbr.org/2016/06/resilience-is-about-how-you-recharge-not-how-you-endure.

27. Joann Deak in a lecture given at the Gardner Carney Leadership Lab Conference, June 17, 2012.

28. Amy Blankson, "How Technology Can Be Part of a Happy Life," *Greater Good Magazine*, May 20, 2021. https://greatergood.berkeley.edu/article/item/how_technology_can_be_part_of_a_happy_life.

29. Jessica Fries-Gaither, Interview by Heidi Kasevich, August 5, 2020.

30. Sir Ken Robertson, "Do Schools Kill Creativity?" *Ted2006*, February 2006, https://www.ted.com/talks/sir_ken_robinson_do_schools_kill_creativity?language=en.

31. Scott Barry Kaufman, *Wired to Create* (New York: Random House, 2015), 44–57.

32. Kaufman, *Wired to Create*, 44–57.

33. Gareth Cook, "The Power of Introverts: A Manifesto for Quiet Brilliance," *Scientific American*, January 24, 2012, https://www.scientificamerican.com/article/the-power-of-introverts/.

34. Daniel J Levitin, "Why the Modern World is Bad for Your Brain," *The Guardian*, January 18, 2015, https://www.theguardian.com/science/2015/jan/18/modern-world-bad-for-brain-daniel-j-levitin-organized-mind-information-overload.

35. Mihaly Csikszentmihalyi, "Flow, The Secret to Happiness," *Ted2004*, February 2004, https://www.ted.com/talks/mihaly_csikszentmihalyi_flow_the_secret_to_happiness.

36. K. Anders Ericsson, Ralf T. Krampe, and Clemens Tesch-Römer, "The Role of Deliberate Practice in the Acquisition of Expert Performance," *Psychological Review* 100, no. 3 (1993): 363–406, https://doi.org/10.1037/0033-295x.100.3.363.

37. Quiet Leadership Institute, "The Road to Extraordinary," *Quiet Revolution*, May 31, 2016, https://www.quietrev.com/the-road-to-extraordinary/.

38. Jenny Anderson, "How to Make Your Kid Good at Anything, According to a World Expert on Peak Performance," *Quartz*, March 14, 2017, https://qz.com/915646/how-to-make-your-kid-good-at-anything-according-to-anders-ericsson-an-expert-on-peak-performance-and-originator-of-the-10000-hour-rule#:~:text=The%20professor%20has%20found%20that,that%20practice%20rewires%20the%20brain.https://qz.com/915646/how-to-make-your-kid-good-at-anything-according-to-anders-ericsson-an-expert-on-peak-performance-and-originator-of-the-10000-hour-rule/.

39. Sam Kane, Interview by Heidi Kasevich, June 29, 2020.

CHAPTER 8

1. Amelia Harper, "Do Open Office Plans Really Work?" *K-12 Dive*, October 4, 2018, https://www.k12dive.com/news/do-open-plan-schools-really-work/538788/.

2. Steve Drummond, "Open Schools Made Noise in the '70s; Now They're Just Noisy," *National Public Radio*, March 27, 2017, https://www.npr.org/sections/ed/2017/03/27/520953343/open-schools-made-noise-in-the-70s-now-theyre-just-noisy.

3. Rob Cross, Reb Rebele, and Adam Grant, "Collaborative Overload," January-February 2016, https://hbr.org/2016/01/collaborative-overload.

4. Marti Olsen Laney, *The Introvert Advantage: How Quiet People Can Thrive in an Extroverted World* (New York: Workman Publishing Company, Inc., 2002), 267.

Russell G. Geen, "Preferred Stimulation Levels in Introverts and Extroverts: Effects on Arousal and Performance," *Journal of Personality and Social Psychology* 46, no. 6 (1984): 1,303-1,312. 6.   Carrie Green, Interview by Heidi Kasevich, August 27, 2020.

7. Richard Louv, *Last Child in the Woods, Saving Our Children from Nature-Deficit Disorder* (Chapel Hill, NC: Algonquin Books of Chapel Hill, 2005), 49; 103.

8. Bonnie Peters, RA, "Biophilic Design in the Learning Environment," *Insights, DRA*, November 30, 2018, https://www.draws.com/biophilic-design-in-the-learning-environment/.

9. Patty Hans, Interview by Heidi Kasevich, June 18, 2020.

10. Sam Kane, Interview by Heidi Kasevich, June 29, 2020.

11. Carrie Green, Interview by Heidi Kasevich, August 27, 2020.

12. Annie Ruefle, Interview by Heidi Kasevich, August 14, 2020.

13. Britt Anderson, Interview by Heidi Kasevich, June 12, 2020.
14. Charlotte Stiverson, Interview by Heidi Kasevich, June 10, 2020.
15. Courtney E. Ackerman, MA, "What Is Kaplan's Attention Restoration Theory (ART)?," *Positive Psychology.com*, November 13, 2018, https://positivepsychology.com/attention-restoration-theory/.
16. Mary Yockey, Interview by Heidi Kasevich, June 18, 2020.
17. Nicole Celestine, "What is Mental Contrasting and How Can We Benefit from It?" *PositivePsychology.com*, January 1, 2020, https://positivepsychology.com/mental-contrasting/.
18. Imke Kriste, Zeina Nicola, Golo Kronenberg, Tara Walker, Robert Liu, and Gerd Kempermann, "Is Silence Golden? Effects of Auditory Stimuli and Their Absence on Adult Hippocampal Neurogenesis," December 1, 2013, https://www.researchgate.net/publication/259110014_Is_silence_golden_Effects_of_auditory_stimuli_and_their_absence_on_adult_hippocampal_neurogenesis.
19. Betsy Gugle, interview by Heidi Kasevich, June 9, 2020.

CHAPTER 9

1. Greg Bamford and Carla Silver, "How Schools Talk about and Notice School Culture," *NAIS*, Spring 2022, https://www.nais.org/magazine/independent-school/spring-2022/how-schools-talk-about-and-notice-school-culture/.
2. Susan Cain, Quiet Schools Network, Quiet Revolution, 2016.
3. Ally Leonard, Interview by Heidi Kasevich, September 17, 2020.
4. Ally Leonard, Interview by Heidi Kasevich, September 17, 2020.
5. Betsy Gugle, Interview by Heidi Kasevich, June 9, 2020.
6. Britt Anderson, Interview by Heidi Kasevich, June 12, 2020.
7. Britt Anderson, Interview by Heidi Kasevich, June 12, 2020.
8. Matthew Williams, Interview by Heidi Kasevich, June 22, 2020.
9. Matthew Williams, Interview by Heidi Kasevich, June 22, 2020.

Additional Resources and Support

Here are additional resources and support to help you on your journey as a Quiet Ambassador:

1. Free Additional Resources: Download additional activities, tools, and case studies for building introvert-friendly classrooms and nurturing quiet leaders at kaseleadership.com/resources.
2. Professional Development: Kase Leadership offers interactive workshops for schools and organizations seeking to create an inclusive leadership culture. See kaseleadership.com for more information.
3. Keynote Speaking: Kase Leadership offers presentations for schools and organizations on the power of quiet leadership. See kaseleadership.com for more information.
4. 1:1 Leadership Coaching: Kase Leadership offers individual coaching for adults of all personality styles seeking to tap into their strengths, stretch outside their comfort zones, set core personal project goals, and build their leadership skills. See kaseleadership.com for more information.

Bibliography

Achor, Shawn and Michelle Gielen. "Resilience Is About How You Recharge, Not How You Endure." *Harvard Business Review*. June 24, 2016. https://hbr.org/2016/06/resilience-is-about-how-you-recharge-not-how-you-endure.

Ackerman, Courtney E. MA. "What Is Kaplan's Attention Restoration Theory (ART)?." *Positive Psychology.com*. November 13, 2018. https://positivepsychology.com/attention-restoration-theory/.

Anderson, Britt. Interview by Heidi Kasevich. June 12, 2020.

Anderson, Jenny. "How to Make Your Kid Good at Anything, According to a World Expert on Peak Performance." *Quartz*. March 14, 2017. https://qz.com/915646/how-to-make-your-kid-good-at-anything-according-to-anders-ericsson-an-expert-on-peak-performance-and-originator-of-the-10000-hour-rule#:~:text=The%20professor%20has%20found%20that,that%20practice%20rewires%20the%20brain.https://qz.com/915646/how-to-make-your-kid-good-at-anything-according-to-anders-ericsson-an-expert-on-peak-performance-and-originator-of-the-10000-hour-rule/.

Ashton, Michael C., Kibeom Lee, and Sampo V. Paunonen. "What Is the Central Feature of Extraversion? Social Attention versus Reward Sensitivity." *Journal of Personality and Social Psychology* 83, no. 1 (2002): 245–252. https://doi.org/10.1037/0022-3514.83.1.245.

Bamford, Greg and Carla Silver. "How Schools Talk about and Notice School Culture." *NAIS*. Spring 2022. https://www.nais.org/magazine/independent-school/spring-2022/how-schools-talk-about-and-notice-school-culture/.

Banaji, M. R. and Anthony G. Greenwald. *Blindspot: Hidden Biases of Good People*. New York: Bantam Books, 2016.

Bechtle, Mike. "Are You Talking to an Extrovert or an Introvert?" *mikebechtle.com*. https://www.mikebechtle.com/are-you-talking-to-an-extrovert-or-an-introvert/.

Berns, Gregory S. et al. "Neurobiological Correlates of Social Conformity and Independence During Mental Rotation." *Society of Biological Psychiatry*. Last modified 2005. http://www.ccnl.emory.edu/greg/Berns%20Conformity%20final%20printed.pdf.

Besant, Hanisha. "The Journey of Brainstorming." *Journal of transformative Innovation* 1, no. 2 (2016): 1–7.

Blankson, Amy. "How Technology Can Be Part of a Happy Life." *Greater Good Magazine.* May 20, 2021.

Boonisar, Derek. Interview by Heidi Kasevich. June 26, 2020.

Brooks, Arthur C. "How the Modern World Made Cowards of Us All." *The New York Times.* July 21, 2017. https://www.nytimes.com/2017/07/21/opinion/how-the-modern-world-made-cowards-of-us-all.html?searchResultPosition=1.

Cain, Susan. "Shyness: An Evolutionary Tactic?" *The New York Times.* June 25, 2011. https://www.nytimes.com/2011/06/26/opinion/sunday/26shyness.html.

Cain, Susan. *Quiet: The Power of Introverts in a World That Can't Stop Talking.* New York: Crown Publishing Group, 2012.

Cain, Susan. *Quiet Revolution Study.* 2014. https://quietrev.com/resources-for-schools/.

Cain, Susan. "The Long Runway." *Quiet, the Power of Introverts Podcast/Panoply/Quiet Revolution.* February 3, 2016. https://susancain.net/susan-cain-quiet-podcast/.

Cain, Susan. *Quiet Ambassador Program.* Quiet Schools Network. 2016.

Celestine, Nicole. "What is Mental Contrasting and How Can We Benefit from It?" *Positive Psychology.com.* January 1, 2020. https://positivepsychology.com/mental-contrasting/.

Cook, Gareth. "The Power of Introverts: A Manifesto for Quiet Brilliance." *Scientific American.* January 24, 2012. https://www.scientificamerican.com/article/the-power-of-introverts/.

Cross, Ethan. *Chatter: The Voice in our Head, Why it Matters, and How to Harness It.* New York: Crown, 2021.

Cross, Rob, Reb Rebele, and Adam Grant. "Collaborative Overload." January-February, 2016. https://hbr.org/2016/01/collaborative-overload.

Csikszentmihalyi, Mihaly. "Flow, The Secret to Happiness." *Ted2004.* February 2004. https://www.ted.com/talks/mihaly_csikszentmihalyi_flow_the_secret_to_happiness.

Cuddy, Amy. *Presence: Bringing Your Boldest Self to Your Biggest Challenges.* Boston, MA: Little, Brown Spark, 2018.

Dahl, Melissa. "How Prolonged Exposure to Sweet, Blessed Silence Benefits the Brain." *New York.* July 8, 2016. https://www.thecut.com/2016/07/scientists-are-discovering-the-neural-benefits-of-silence.html.

Dahl, Roald. *Matilda.* New York: Viking, 1988.

Davidson, Bernard, Ralph A. Gillies, and Allen L. Pelletier. "Introversion and Medical Student Education: Challenges for Both Students and Educators." *Teaching and Learning in Medicine* 27, no. 1 (February 2015): 99–104, https://doi.org/10.1080/10401334.2014.979183.

Davis, Janetta. Interview by Heidi Kasevich. August 4, 2020.

Deak, JoAnn. Lecture at Gardner Carney Leadership Lab Conference. June 17, 2012.

Dembling, Sophia. *The Introverts Way: Living a Quiet Life in a Noisy World.* New York: Penguin Group, 2012.

Dowell, Rance G. and D. Tomlin. "The Effect of the Classroom Environment on Literacy Development." *NPJ Science of Learning* 8, no. 9 (2023). https://doi.org/10.1038/s41539-023-00157-y.

Drummond, Steve. "Open Schools Made Noise in the '70s; Now They're Just Noisy." *National Public Radio.* March 27, 2017. https://www.npr.org/sections/ed/2017/03/27/520953343/open-schools-made-noise-in-the-70s-now-theyre-just-noisy.

Emre, Merve. *The Personality Brokers: the Strange History of Myers-Briggs and the Birth of Personality Testing.* Toronto: Vintage Canada, 2019.

Ericsson, K. Anders, Ralf T. Krampe, and Clemens Tesch-Römer. "The Role of Deliberate Practice in the Acquisition of Expert Performance." *Psychological Review* 100, no. 3 (1993): 363–406. https://doi.org/10.1037/0033-295x.100.3.363.

Eysenck, Sybil B. G. and H. J. Eysenck. "Salivary Response to Lemon Juice as a Measure of Introversion." *The Measurement of Personality* (1976): 87–93. https://doi.org/10.1007/978-94-011-6168-8_10.

Fish, Ted. Interview by Heidi Kasevich. June 18, 2020.

Fonseca, Christine. *Quiet Kids - Help Your Introverted Child Succeed in an Extroverted World.* Waco, TX: Prufrock Press Inc., 2014.

Fries-Gaither, Jessica. Interview by Heidi Kasevich. August 5, 2020.

Fuglei, Monica. "Unconscious Discrimination: How to Defeat Four Hidden Teacher Biases." *Resilient Educator.* Last modified September 7, 2018. https://education.cu-portland.edu/blog/classroom-resources/unconscious-discrimination-avoiding-teacher-biases.

Geen, Russell G. "Preferred Stimulation Levels in Introverts and Extroverts: Effects on Arousal and Performance." *Journal of Personality and Social Psychology* 46, no. 6. (1984): 1,303–1,312.

Gino, Francesca. *Sidetracked: Why Our Decisions Get Derailed, and How We Can Stick to the Plan.* Boston, MA: Harvard Business Review Press, 2013.

Godsey, Michael. "Teaching: Not for Introverts." *Atlantic Media Company.* January 25, 2016. https://www.theatlantic.com/education/archive/2016/01/why-introverted-teachers-are-burning-out/425151/.

Granneman, Jennifer. "Why Introverts and Extroverts Are Different: The Science." *Quiet Revolution.* Last modified December 21, 2015. https://www.quietrev.com/why-introverts-and-extroverts-are-different-the-science/.

Grant, Adam, Francesca Gino, and David A. Hofmann, "Reversing the Extraverted Leadership Advantage: The Role of Employee Proactivity." *Academy of Management* (June 2011). https://journals.aom.org/doi/10.5465/amj.2011.61968043

Grant, Adam. "5 Myths About Introverts and Extroverts." *Quiet Revolution.* September 23, 2015, https://www.quietrev.com/5-myths-about-introverts-and-extroverts/.

Grant, Adam. "WorkLife." *WorkLife. TED.* 2018. https://www.ted.com/podcasts/worklife.

Grant, Adam. "Say Goodbye to MBTI, the Fad That Won't Die." *LinkedIn.* Accessed November 21, 2019. https://www.linkedin.com/pulse/20130917155206-69244073-say-goodbye-to-mbti-the-fad-that-won-t-die.

Grant, Adam. "Why Brainstorming Doesn't Work." *Time*. October 24, 2023. https://time.com/6327515/brainstorming-doesnt-work-essay/.

Green, Carrie. Interview by Heidi Kasevich. August 27, 2020.

Greenleaf, Robert. *The Servant as Leader.* The Greenleaf Center for Servant Leadership, 2015.

Gross, Daniel. "This is Your Brain on Silence." *Nautilus*. July 13, 2014. https://nautil.us/this-is-your-brain-on-silence-235023/.

"Groupthink." *Psychology Today*. https://www.psychologytoday.com/us/basics/groupthink.

Gruenfeld, Deborah. "Power and Influence." Stanford University. *VMware Women's Leadership Innovation Lab*. https://womensleadership.stanford.edu/resources/voice-influence/power-influence.

Gugle, Betsy. Interview by Heidi Kasevich. June 9, 2020.

Hans, Patty. Interview by Heidi Kasevich. June 18, 2020.

Harper, Amelia. "Do Open Office Plans Really Work?" *K-12 Dive*. October 4, 2018. https://www.k12dive.com/news/do-open-plan-schools-really-work/538788/.

Hawkins, Aniele. Interview by Heidi Kasevich. August 21, 2020.

Helgoe, Laurie. "Revenge of the Introvert." *Psychology Today*. Accessed November 21, 2019. https://www.psychologytoday.com/us/articles/201009/revenge-the-introvert.

Hendriksen, Ellen. "The 4 Differences Between Introversion and Social Anxiety." *Quiet Revolution*. Last modified May 20, 2016. https://www.quietrev.com/the-4-differences-between-introversion-and-social-anxiety/.

Herman, Amy E. *Visual Intelligence.* New York: Houghton-Mifflin, 2016.

Hinds, Andy. "The World's Richest Introvert." *Quiet Revolution*. August 6, 2023, https://quietrev.com/warren-buffett/.

Howard, Rick and Maeve McKillen. "Extraversion and Performance in the Perceptual Maze Test." *Personality and Individual Differences* 11, no. 4 (1990): 391–396. https://doi.org/10.1016/0191-8869(90)90221-C.

"Humility." *Values in Action Institute on Character.* https://www.viacharacter.org/character-strengths/humility.

Hurst, Kelly Wickam. "Quiet Black Girls - And How We Fail Them," *Quiet Revolution*. https://quietrev.com/quiet-black-girls-and-how-we-fail-them/.

Jennings, Patricia A. *Mindfulness for Teachers: Simple Skill for Peace and Productivity in the Classroom.* New York: W & W Norton and Company, 2015.

Johnson, Miranda. "The Qualities of an Introverted Leader." *Quiet Diarist - Quiet Revolution*. https://quietrev.com/quiet_diaries/the-qualities-of-an-introverted-leader/.

Jorgenson, Olaf. "The Parent-School Partnership: Optimizing Relationships and Building Understanding." *NAIS*. Last modified January 31, 2023. https://www.nais.org/learn/independent-ideas/january-2023/the-parent-school-partnership-optimizing-relationships-and-building-understanding/?utm_source=bn&utm_medium=email&utm_campaign=mc&utm_content=ltc.

Jung, C.G. *Psychological Types.* Zurich: Rascher Verlag, 1921.

Kagan, Jerome and Nancy C. Snidman. *The Long Shadow of Temperament.* Cambridge, MA: Harvard University Press, 2009.

Kane, Sam. Interview by Heidi Kasevich. June 29, 2020.
Kaufman, Scott Barry. "Will the Real Introverts Please Stand Up?" *Scientific American Blog Network*. Last modified June 9, 2014. https://blogs.scientificamerican.com/beautiful-minds/will-the-real-introverts-please-stand-up?.
Kaufman, Scott Barry. *Wired to Create*. New York: Random House, 2015.
Kaufman, Scott Barry. "How to Change Your Personality," *The Atlantic. Atlantic Media Company*. Last modified July 30, 2016. https://www.theatlantic.com/health/archive/2016/07/can-personality-be-changed/492956/.
Kaufman, Scott Barry. "The Real Science of Introversion (and the Rest of Personality)." *Scientific American Blog Network*. Last modified December 7, 2015. https://blogs.scientificamerican.com/beautiful-minds/the-real-science-of-introversion-and-the-rest-of-personality/.
Kesebir, Pelin and Selin Kesebir. "The Cultural Salience of Moral Character and Virtue Declined in Twentieth Century America." *Journal of Positive Psychology*. November 2012. https://doi.org/10.1080/17439760.2016.1167940.
Kriste, Imke, Zeina Nicola, Golo Kronenberg, Tara Walker, Robert Liu, and Gerd Kempermann. "Is Silence Golden? Effects of Auditory Stimuli and Their Absence on Adult Hippocampal Neurogenesis." December 1, 2013. https://www.researchgate.net/publication/259110014_Is_silence_golden_Effects_of_auditory_stimuli_and_their_absence_on_adult_hippocampal_neurogenesis.
Laney, Marti Olsen. *The Introvert Advantage*. New York: Workman Publishing, 2002.
Laney, Marti Olsen, Psy.D. *The Hidden Gifts of the Introverted Child - Helping Your Child Thrive in an Extroverted World*. New York: Workman Publishing Company, Inc., 2005.
Larson, Reed W. "The Emergence of Solitude as a Constructive Domain of Experience in Early Adolescence." *Society for Research in Child Development*. June 30, 2006. https://doi.org/10.1111/j.1467-8624.1997.tb01927.x.
"Lemon Juice Introversion Test." *Psychologist World*. https://www.psychologistworld.com/influence-personality/introversion-extraversion-lemon-juice-test.
Leonard, Ally. Interview by Heidi Kasevich. September 17, 2020.
Levitin, Daniel J. "Why the Modern World is Bad for Your Brain." *The Guardian*. January 18, 2015. https://www.theguardian.com/science/2015/jan/18/modern-world-bad-for-brain-daniel-j-levitin-organized-mind-information-overload.
Lightner, Judy and LeighAnn Tomaswick. "Teachiing Tools in a Flash, Active Learning - Think, Pair, Share." *Kent State University, Center for Teaching and Learning*. Last modified February 1, 2017. https://www-s3-live.kent.edu/s3fs-root/s3fs-public/file/Teaching%20Tools%20in%20A%20Flash%20-%20Think%2C%20Pair%2C%20Share%20%20-%20Final.pdf?VersionId=I1tG2t8a9oi_cwhe_4U5V3u0Qc7emXPU.
Lippman, Walter. *Public Opinion*. Brace and Company, 1922.
Little, Brian R. "Acting Out of Character in the Imortal Profession: Toward a Free Trait Agreement." *Academic Matters*. April-May 2010. https://www.brianrlittle.com/articles/acting-out-of-character-in-the-immortal-profession-toward-a-free-trait-

Little, Brian R. "Personal Projects and Free Traits: Personality and Motivation Reconsidered," *Admin*. Last modified October 24, 2011. https://www.brianrlittle.com/articles/ personal-projects-and-free-traits/.

Little, Brian R. *Me, Myself, and Us: The Science of Personality and the Art of Well-Being*. New York: Public Affairs, 2014.

Little, Brian R. "How Your To-Do List Shapes Your Personality — and How to Use It to Remake Who You Are." *Ideas.Ted.Com*. Last modified August 15, 2017. https://ideas.ted.com/how-our-projects-shape-our-personalities-and-how-we-can-use-them-to-remake-who-we-are/.

Louv, Richard. *Last Child in the Woods, Saving Our Children from Nature-Deficit Disorder*. Chapel Hill, NC: Algonquin Books of Chapel Hill, 2005.

Magee, Joanne. Interview by Heidi Kasevich. April 29, 2019.

McGowan, Sean Patrick. Interview by Heidi Kasevich. April 13, 2019.

Milne, A.A. *The Complete Tales of Winnie-the-Pooh*. New York: Dutton Children's Books, 1994.

Mind Tools Content Team. "Brainwriting." *MindTools*. https://www.mindtools.com/ak3qj17/brainwriting

Owens, Bradley and David Hekman. "Modeling How to Grow: An Inductive Examination of Humble Leader Behavior, Contingencies, and Outcomes." *Academy of Management Journal* 55, no. 4 (April 2012): 787–818.

Pavot, William, Ed Diener, and Frank Fujita. "Extraversion and Happiness." *Personality and Individual Differences* 11, no. 12 (1990): 1299–1306. https://doi.org/10.1016/0191-8869(90)90157-m.

"Perspective." *Values in Action Institute on Character*. https://www.viacharacter.org/character-strengths/humility.

Peters, Bonnie RA. "Biophilic Design in the Learning Environment." *Insights. DRA*. November 30, 2018. https://www.draws.com/biophilic-design-in-the-learning-environment/.

Polivy, Janet and C. Peter Herman. "Dieting and Binging: A Causal Analysis." *American Psychologist* 40, no. 2 (1985): 193–201. https://doi.org/10.1037/0003-066x.40.2.193.

Porter, Tenelle. "The Benefits of Admitting When You Don't Know." *Greater Good Magazine*. Last modified July 16, 2018, https://greatergood.berkeley.edu/article/item/the_benefits_of_admitting_when_you_dont_know.

Prime, Jeanine and Elizabeth Salib. "The Best Leaders Are Humble Leaders." *Harvard Business Review*. Last modified May 12, 2014. https://hbr.org/2014/05/the-best-leaders-are-humble-leaders.

Quiet Leadership Institute. "The Road to Extraordinary." *Quiet Revolution*. May 31, 2016. https://www.quietrev.com/the-road-to-extraordinary/.

Resch, Linda. Interview by Heidi Kasevich. July 29, 2020.

Robertson, Sir Ken. "Do Schools Kill Creativity?" *Ted 2006*. February 2006, https://www.ted.com/talks/sir_ken_robinson_do_schools_kill_creativity?language=en.

Rowe, Mary Budd. "Wait Time and Rewards as Instructional Variables." *ERIC Clearinghouse for Social Studies/Social Science Education*. April 1972. https://archive.org/details/ERIC_ED061103.

Ruefle, Annie. Interview by Heidi Kasevich. August 14, 2020.
Saad, Lydia. "Americans Have Close But Wary Bond With Their Smartphone." *Gallup*. June 20, 2022. https://news.gallup.com/poll/393785/americans-close-wary-bond-smartphone.aspx.
Schwartz, Carl E. and Susan Cain, "Quiet Revolution," *Quiet Revolution*. Panoply. Last modified June 15, 2016.
Schwartz, Carl E., Nancy C. Snidman, and Jerome Kagan. "Adolescent Social Anxiety as an Outcome of Inhibited Temperament in Childhood." *Journal of the American Academy of Child & Adolescent Psychiatry* 38, no. 8 (1999): 1008–1015. https://doi.org/10.1097/00004583-199908000-00017.
Selover, Casey. Interview by Heidi Kasevich. August 21, 2020.
Senechal, Diana. *Republic of Noise: The Loss of Solitude in Schools and Culture*. Lanham, MD: Rowman & Littlefield, 2012.
Shrum, Judith L. "Wait Time and Student Performance Level in Second Language Classrooms." *The Journal of Classroom Interaction* 20, no. 1 (1984): 29–35. http://www.jstor.org/stable/43997866.
Smith, Robin. Interview by Heidi Kasevich. September 16, 2020.
Stahl, Robert J. "Using 'Think-Time' and 'Wait-Time' Skillfully in the Classroom." *ERIC Clearinghouse for Social Studies/Social Science Education*. May 1954. http://ocw.umb.edu/early-education-development/echd-440-640-eec-language-and-literacy-course/learning-module-1/module-5/Wait%20Time.pdf.
Stiverson, Charlotte. Conversation with Heidi Kasevich. February 15, 2023.
Stiverson, Charlotte. Interview by Heidi Kasevich. June 10, 2020.
Susman, Warren I. *Culture as History: the Transformation of American Society in the Twentieth Century*. Washington, DC: Smithsonian Inst. Press, 2003.
Szegedy-Maszak, Marianne. "As Noise Rises, so Do the Dangers." *Los Angeles Times*. Last modified November 28, 2005. https://www.latimes.com/archives/la-xpm-2005-nov-28-he-noise28-story.html.
Tartakovsky, Margarita. "Seven Persistent Myths about Introverts and Extroverts." *Psych Central*. Last modified September 11, 2013. https://psychcentral.com/blog/7-persistent-myths-about-introverts-extroverts#1.
Thompson, Leigh. "How Brainwriting can get Better Ideas out of your Team." *Harvard Business Review*. May 16, 2017. https://hbr.org/sponsored/2017/05/how-brainwriting-can-get-better-ideas-out-of-your-team.
Tolkein, J.R.R. *The Fellowship of the Ring*. New York: Ballantine Books, Inc., 1965.
Tolkein, J.R.R. *The Hobbit*. New York: Ballantine Books, Inc., 1966.
Waldeck, Jen. Interview by Heidi Kasevich. June 19, 2020.
Whitehead, Nadia. "People Would Rather be Electrically Shocked than Left Alone with Their Thoughts." *Science*. July 3, 2014. https://www.science.org/doi/10.1126/science.1250830.
Wielgus, Margot, Thomas Böhm, and Günter Figal. "Solitude & Thinking: Henry David Thoreau." In *Anthropologie Der Theorie*, edited by Thomas Jürgasch and Tobias Keiling, 209–224. Mohr Siebeck GmbH and Co. KG, 2017. http://www.jstor.org/stable/j.ctvrs90hh.12.
Williams, Matthew. Interview by Heidi Kasevich. June 22, 2020.

Wilson, Kim. Interview by Heidi Kasevich. August 11, 2020.
Wood, Patti. "The Body Language of Listening." *pattiwood.net.* http://www.patti-wood.net/article.asp?PageID=2323.
Wright, Jennifer Cole. "The Psychological Significance of Humility." *Journal of Positive Psychology.* April 22, 2016. https://doi.org/10.1080/17439760.2016.1167940.
Yockey, Mary. Interview by Heidi Kasevich. June 18, 2020.
Zakrzewski, Vicki. "How to Cultivate Humble Leadership." *Greater Good Magazine.* Last modified February 2016. https://greatergood.berkeley.edu/article/item/how_to_cultivate_humble_leadership.
Zenger, Jack and Joseph Folkman. "What Great Listeners Actually Do." *Harvard Business Review.* Last modified July 14, 2016. https://hbr.org/2016/07/what-great-listeners-actually-do.
Zorn, Justin and Leigh Marz. *Golden: The Power of Silence in a World of Noise.* New York: HarperCollins, 2022.
Zorn, Justin, and Leigh Marz. "How to Build a Culture that Honors Quiet Time." *Harvard Business Review.* May 24, 2022. https://hbr.org/2022/05/how-to-build-a-culture-that-honors-quiet-time.

Index

Achor, Shawn, 96
active listening, 51–53, 59
adaptability, 35–36
Adler, Alfred, 7
alone time, 4, 7, 11, 25, 77, 89, 93, 95, 99
ambiverts, 12, 22–23
anecdotal comments, 69
anti-anxiety drug, 7
antisocial, 3, 7–11, 93, 97, 106
Ashton, Michael, 22
automatic associations, 8
awareness, 8–10, 12, 79, 110

Bamford, Greg, 117
Berns, Gregory, 67
Blankson, Amy, 97
Blindspot: The Hidden Biases of Good People, 8
Bock, Laszlo, 27
Bohn, Thomas, 91
Book Club, 76, 79, 83, 86
brainstorming strategies, 66–69
brainwriting, 68
Briggs, Katherine, 18
Brooks, Arthur C., 29
Buffett, Warren, 28
burnout, 5, 35, 103

Cain, Susan, 26, 37
channels of communication, 51–52
character, 5
character strengths, 26–27, 32
classroom engagement, ix, 51
classroom layout, 104–6
coaching, 41, 42, 121
cognitive empathy, 13–14
collaborative learning, ix
communication "toolkits," 76
core personal projects, 35–36, 38, 39, 44
creativity, 50, 66, 68, 97–98, 101, 107
Cross, Rob, 104
Csikszentmihalyi, Mihaly, 98
Cuddy, Amy, 52
cultural norms, 7, 51
culture values, 7

Dahl, Roald, 81
deep listening, ix, 51
deliberate practice, 98, 99
deliberation, 7
Dembling, Sophia, 7
Diagnostic and Statistical Manual, the DSM-IV, 7
disrupting bias, 16
diversity, equity and inclusion, 119–20

Dowell, Richard C., 91
dynamic personality, 5

emotions, 28
Emre, Merve, 6
engagement, 49–60; nonverbal engagement, 51–53; verbal engagement, 54–57
equity, 119–20
Ericsson, K. Anders, 98
expectation, 58–60
extroversion, 3
extrovert, 29; adaptability, 35–36; bias, strategies for, 12–14; cultural origins of, 5–6; ideal, 14–15; learning style, 51; MBTI, 18; modification of, 25–28; origins of, 6–7; personality preferences, 31; reflective pausing, 63–65; sensitivity to rewards, 22; social and sensory stimuli, 21; social attention, 3
extrovert bias, 12–14, 120
extrovert ideal, 5–7, 14–15
Eysenck, Hans, 19

faculty spaces, 107–8, 113
family gatherings at school, 20
family reading at home, 80
Figal, Gunter, 91
fixed traits, 35
Fonseca, Christine, 77
"free trait agreement", 42–43
free traits, 23, 30, 35
Freud, Sigmund, 7
Fuglei, Monica, 9

garden, 110, 111
Geen, Russell, 105
Gielan, Michelle, 96
goal identification, 37
Godsey, Michael, 4
Granneman, Jennifer, 22
Grant, Adam, 18, 22, 28, 104
Greenleaf, Robert, 27

Gross, Daniel A., 92
groupthink, 66
group work, 70, 72

Harper, Amelia, 103
Hekman, David, 27
Helgoe, Laurie, 9
Hendriksen, Ellen, 9
Herman, Peter, 36
The Hobbit, 82
Howard, Rick, 68
humility, 27
Hurst, Kelly Wickham, 8

implicit bias, 7–9, 15; culture values, 7; stereotypes, 8–9
inclusion approach, 119–20
introspection, 7
introverted educator, 5, 43, 93
introvert-extrovert personality preferences indicator for adults and teens, 23–27
introvert-friendly educator, 96, 107, 108
introverts, 29; adaptability, 35–36; alone time, require of, 4; antisocial, narcissistic behavior, 7; character strengths, 26–27, 32; common misperceptions, 15; communication and problem-solving style, 61; detriment of, 3; extroverts, 12; feel abnormal, 4; inferiority complex, 7; learning style, 51; Long Runway approach, 62–63; lose confidence, 4; MBTI, 18; misperceptions about, 9–11; modification of, 25–26; pedagogical strategy, 66; perceive, 13; personality-diverse communities, 30; personality preferences, 31; perspective, 28; public speaking stretch for, 40–42; recharging time for, 5; reflective pausing, 63–65; sensitivity to stimulation, 19–21; stressed out, anxious, or depressed, 4
The Introvert's Way, 7

Johnson, John, 26
Jung, Carl, 6, 7

Kagan, Jerome, 20
Kaplan, Rachel, 111
Kaufman, Scott Barry, 19, 22, 27, 98
Kettert, Steven, 106
kindness, 69
Kirste, Imke, 92, 112

Laney, Marti Olsen, 7, 22, 77
large/small group discussions, 60
leadership program approach, 118–19
learning style, 51
Lee, Kibeom, 22
Lemon Juice Introversion Test, 20
lending library, 83
Lippman, Walter, 8
Little, Brian, 35
Long Runway approach, 62–63, 71
Louv, Richard, 106
Lyman, Frank, 65

Mahatma Gandhi, 35
Marz, Leigh, 89
mastery, 98–99, 101–2
Matilda, 81
McKillen, Maeve, 68
memory, 92, 112
micro-mindful moments, 30, 43–44, 58, 71, 84, 100, 112–13
mindset shift, 13
misperceptions of introverts, 9–11, 15
modification of personality preferences indicator for younger students, 25–26
Myers, Isabel Briggs, 18
Myers–Briggs Type Indicator (MBTI), 18

nervous systems, 4
neurobiology, 12, 14, 20
neurotransmitters, 22
noise, 100–101
nonverbal engagement: active listening, 51–53; written reflections, 54–56

one-on-one coaching approach, 121
open education, 103
Open Education Movement, 103
open plan classroom, 91, 103
Osborn, Alex, 66
Owens, Bradley, 27

parasympathetic system, 22
parent-school partnerships: about introverted children, 76–77, 85; elementary and middle school literature, 81–82; family book club, 79–80, 86; forging, 85; honest feedback, 75; long runway for social events, 79, 85; middle-and high-school literature, 82; parental complaints, 75; preschool and elementary school literature, 80–81; quiet spaces at home, 77–79; routine structure, 77; school-sponsored book club, 83; school-sponsored quiet coffees, 83–84
participation, 3, 4, 49–51, 56–58, 67
Paunonen, Sampo, 22
personal interviews, x
personality, 5
The Personality Brokers, 6
Personality Preferences Indicator, 23
personality types, 68
perspective, 28, 57
Polivy, Janet, 36
power of conformity, 67
premature consensus, 67
progress reports approach, 120–21
prudence, 28–30
Psychological Types, 6
public speaking stretch, 40–42

quiet ambassadors, 121–22
quiet-friendly comments, 69, 72–73; group work, 72; Long Runway approach, 71–72; reflective pausing, 72
quiet initiatives, x, 117, 118, 120
quiet leadership, xi, 29, 118

quiet revolution, 19, 20, 26, 120
quiet spaces, in classrooms: faculty spaces, 107–8, 113; nooks and books, 106–7; on and off school grounds, 110–12, 114; school building, 108–10, 113–14; social and sensory stimulation, 104–6

Rance, Gary, 91
Rebele, Reb, 104
recess, 4, 15, 26, 108, 110
recharge time (at school, after school), 5, 79, 93–96, 113–14
recharging styles, 25, 78, 107
reflective pausing, 70, 72
resilience, 96–98
reward sensitivity, 22
routines, 49, 76, 77
Rowe, Mary Budd, 65
rubrics for classroom engagement, 54–57

scaffolding, 44
school building, 108–10, 113–14
school culture, 117
school grounds, 43, 110–12
Schwartz, Carl, 20
Science, 89
self-awareness, 31, 50–51, 57
self-knowledge, 17
self-negation, 37
Senechal, Diana, 91
shyness, 9–10; *vs.* introversion, 7, 10
silence, 49, 51, 61–69, 92–93
Silver, Carla, 117
situational awareness, 31
slowness, 11
social and sensory stimulation, 118
social anxiety, 9
social attention, 10
social events, 18
social identity, 23
social personas, 23
solitude: and creativity, 97–98, 101; and mastery, 98–99, 101–2; as muscle, 112; plenitude solitude, 91–92; recharging time, 93–96, 101; and resilience, 96–97; setting for silence, 92–93, 99–100; solitude muscles, 99, 102
speech over quantity, ix
stereotype, 8, 12
stimulation sensitivity, 19–21, 104–6
stretch: dining hall stretch, 38–40; public speaking stretch, 40–42; stretch meter, 37–40
stretch meter strategy: for extroverts, 37; goal identification, 37; for introverts, 38
Susman, Warren, 5
sympathetic system, 22

talking points with families about introverted children, 76–77, 85
Taoism, viii
Tartakovsky, Margarita, 10
teaching, 49–51
teaching and learning communities, ix–x
temperament: diversity, 17; temperament-inclusivity, 121, 122
temperament-inclusive culture, 118
temperaments, 118
Think, Pair, and Share, 65–66
Thoreau, Henry David, 91
Tomlin, Dani, 91

unconscious biases, 12
The Values in Action Institute on Character, 26–29

verbal engagement, 54–57

wellness approach, 120
Wielgus, Margot, 91
Wilson, E. O., 106
Winnie-the-Pooh, 80
word choices and placement, 12
work spaces, 106–7, 109
writing, ix
written reflections, 59–60

yin/yang symbol, viii, ix

Zorn, Justin, 89

About the Author

Dr. Heidi Kasevich is the founder of Kase Leadership, where she is a leadership educator and executive coach. Through workshops, keynote presentations, and individual and team coaching, she facilitates the courageous conversations needed to create communities of belonging where introverts are as valued as their extroverted counterparts for their potential to learn and lead. She is also the founding director of the Gardner Carney Leadership Institute's School Certification Program, which trains educators to nurture the next generation to be self-aware, humble, resilient, and compassionate leaders.

Kasevich recently served as director of education at Susan Cain's Quiet Revolution, where she launched a national introvert-inclusivity professional development program, featured in numerous national publications. Her proficiency is grounded in over twenty years of experience as a history chair and leadership program designer at several schools and universities in New York City and Paris. She earned her PhD from New York University and is co-author of *The Introverted Actor: Practical Approaches*, which empowers quiet actors to leverage their strengths and navigate all aspects of the profession. She received the Education 2.0 Visionary Leadership award in 2024.

www.ingramcontent.com/pod-product-compliance
Lightning Source LLC
Chambersburg PA
CBHW021145230426
43667CB00005B/255